Andreas Banzerus

Willingness to Accept for Instagram Accounts

First Empirical Evidence

Anchor Academic
Publishing

Banzerus, Andreas: Willingness to Accept for Instagram Accounts. First Empirical Evidence, Hamburg, Anchor Academic Publishing 2016

Buch-ISBN: 978-3-96067-071-1
PDF-eBook-ISBN: 978-3-96067-571-6
Druck/Herstellung: Anchor Academic Publishing, Hamburg, 2016

Bibliografische Information der Deutschen Nationalbibliothek:
Die Deutsche Nationalbibliothek verzeichnet diese Publikation in der Deutschen Nationalbibliografie; detaillierte bibliografische Daten sind im Internet über http://dnb.d-nb.de abrufbar.

Bibliographical Information of the German National Library:
The German National Library lists this publication in the German National Bibliography. Detailed bibliographic data can be found at: http://dnb.d-nb.de

© Anchor Academic Publishing, Imprint der Diplomica Verlag GmbH
Hermannstal 119k, 22119 Hamburg
http://www.diplomica-verlag.de, Hamburg 2016
Printed in Germany

Willingness to Accept for Instagram Accounts:

First Empirical Evidence

Abstract:

Finding an incentive compatible method to assess account values can be seen as the bedrock of social media research across all platforms and is of crucial importance for researches and practitioners alike. This study presents a novel method of applying the willingness to accept instead of the commonly used willingness to pay to establish account values on Instagram, by modifying a randomised Vickrey Auction. Primary research among 1024 participants and 409 Instagram users measured the willingness to accept, in relation to demographic variables, account and interaction metrics. The average account was valued at 100 € median, correlating significantly with participant's income and prevalently with the number of followers. Other significant correlations were found with the duration since sign up, number of posts, average number of likes and comments as well as the decision to establish a micro blogging business. Findings are discussed in regards to limitations and implications for Instagram's business model in terms of a Freemium model, insurances companies offering privacy enhancing features and ad campaign pricing when users engage in brand collaborations.

List of Contents

List of Figures

List of Abbreviations

B_r	Random Bid
B_S	Bid of the Seller
BDM	Becker DeGroot Marschak (Becker et al., 1964)
E	Expected value
HTML	HyperText Markup Language
IQR	Interquartile Range (box plot)
N_F	Number of Instagram Followers
p^*	Optimal price
PSM	Price Sensitivity Meter (van Westendorp, 1976)
RP	Risk Premium
RQ	Research Question
$r_{x;y}$	Correlation between x and y
u_s	Derived Utility of the Seller
v_s	True Value of the Possessed Good (WTA)
WTA	Willingness to Accept
WTP	Willingness to Pay
Δ	Change in two Figures
π	Profit

1 Introduction

The radical novelty of the Web 2.0 has shifted focus from website administration generated content to user generated content and allowed for the emergence of user generated businesses in the same movement. Whilst a vast majority of users can be described as "lurkers" and passive users, following the 1% rule, only one in one hundred people actually actively participated in creating content on the internet ten years ago (van Mierlo, 2014). Fast forward 10 years, the share of active users posting videos, sharing pictures, writing blogs has now risen to 9% in 2009. The emergence of social networks, allowing for more enticing opportunities to interact with other users or brands and low barriers to sharing content over 3G and now 4G technology can be held accountable for this development. In the same period the first incidences of social media entrepreneurship emerged and allowed users to gain revenue from social media sites in return for various forms of advertising and related income sources. The suddenly arising business-critical issues of privacy concerns (e.g. losing the account over unauthorised access or technological errors) and technology based questions have been researched in a platform specific manner, with most research revolving around Twitter and Facebook users. Despite its rapid growth and recent overtake by Facebook, reliable economic studies on social picture sharing service Instagram are not represented in contemporary research. Therefore, this study should serve as the first foundation in this area and analyse the monetary value behind Instagram accounts. By closing this existing research gap, insurances may be able to expand their current range of services and insure Instagram related business models. At the same time, Instagram receives the opportunity to launch a fee-based premium version of their existing platform, which further secures the value and privacy of one account, in the form of a Freemium model. The third beneficiaries of the study are Instagram users, who derive information on how to find the optimal price for sponsored content on the network.

The dominant methodology to determine price preferences, analogous to Facebook or Twitter research, is to statistically determine a users willingness to pay (WTP, purchasing price) to keep and use the existing account, through a survey. Willingness to accept (WTA, selling price) as the slightly higher counterpart mechanism is expected to complement the survey over the endowment effect. The effect postulates that there is a "sentimental" non-rational value attached to the account, overestimating its actual value. Yet the overestimation may drive the price a customer is willing to pay for an insurance and privacy protection (WTA > WTP).

To allow incentive compatible[1] measurement of the WTA (instead of the WTP), the renowned Becker-DeGroot-Marschak mechanism is modified and applied to suit the study requirements. Following data collection all established demographic variables such as age, gender and education and key account metrics such as followers, number of posted pictures shall then be used in a second step to define statistically significant correlations to further break down and define WTA composition.

The scientific approach in measuring account values and metric will allow insight for three main stakeholders of this study: Instagram, may now act as provider of additional security through a Freemium model and thus may be able to secure additional revenue, aside from advertising. Knowing a close to accurate value of a profile insurance companies will be able to insure users and corporate accounts against loss of business and the intellectual property created. Professional social media users, who sustain a significant proportion of their monthly income through Instagram, will be able to determine an adequate market price for advertising opportunities, taking into account positive and negative changes in followers.

In order to diligently and systematically address the below research question this dissertation will be divided into the following conceptual chapters. An analysis of key findings in current literature will allow us to establish an up to date understanding of network industries generally with special focus on social networks, their characteristics, pricing options and applicable mechanism in Chapter 2. Chapter 3 will then justify and design an appropriate research plan, touching upon ethical issues and potential risks and their mitigation during the data collection. When analysing sample data, focus will be set on demographic variables in descriptive statistics and correlations with key account metrics and socio-demographics to develop a round understanding of the topic. Concluding, all findings will be discussed in regards to limitations, implications and potential further research questions.

---

[1] For the individual to disclose their true preferences and values

Explore the following research questions:

RQ1   Mathematically develop an incentive compatible method to expose user's willingness to accept (WTA) for existing Instagram accounts.

RQ2   Calculate descriptive statistics of the willingness to accept (WTA) for existing Instagram accounts.

RQ3   Find significant correlations (to different levels) of the willingness to accept (WTA) with demographic variables and key account metrics in order to investigate the current level of development of businesses on Instagram.

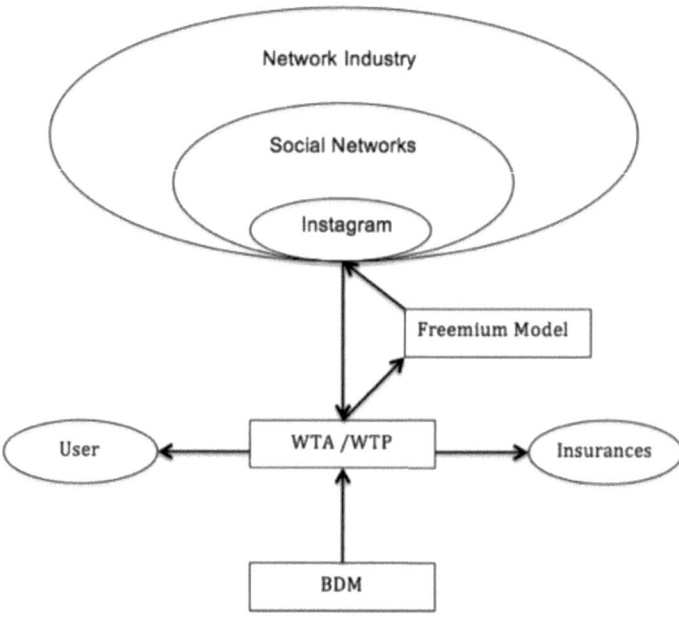

Figure 1: Overview of research fields (own illustration)

2 Literature Review

2.1 Alignment and Social Networks

Past years have seen a trend in the usage of social media platforms, where users are able to interact by self or peer- generated content in a virtual environment (Kaplan and Haenlein, 2010). Traditionally, information in the online context has been shared unidirectional from few content creators to attract are large number of recipients by using simple HTML web pages (Cormode and Krishnamurthy, 2008). Guided by several technological changes and increasing information processing capacity ("Moore's law") of servers since 2004 this proportion has progressively shifted towards the number of content creators (Fox and Pierce, 2009, Kambil, 2008, O'reilly, 2007). In the so-called Web 2.0 era content and information flows differ from previous times as users may contribute to or customise an online service or platform using a profile or personal user account (O'reilly, 2007, Weinberg, 2009). This substantial and on-going change also empowered millions of people to start online businesses that create value by using social media platforms, blogs, video sharing platforms or other web applications characterised through significantly lowering set up costs and barriers to enter an online market than previous offline markets (O'Reilly, 2005). Generally, social media platforms feature the highest diffusion rates among content creators as they aim to target a broad audience with strategic focus on direct network effects (Kietzmann et al., 2011, Lin and Lu, 2011). While "older" networks such as Facebook (established in 2004) and Twitter (established in 2006) have frequently been addressed in studies in the field of social, business and economic science, the novel social picture sharing service Instagram (established in 2010) has been underestimated in its growth potential by researchers in the past. The current growth rates support this hypothesis (Figure 2) and further indicate a knowledge gap in regards to the social network Instagram. In addition, the rise in the Alexa ranking, which can be seen as the dominant web analytical service, of 31 places to position number 26 (19.05.15) highlights the rapid diffusion of Instagram at the moment (Alexa, 2015, Lo and Sedhain, 2006). Bearing that in mind, Instagram may aptly be described by the "Early Majority" phase of the diffusion process, whereby Facebook and Twitter are allocated in the "Late Majority" or in the turning point of Rogers (2010) renowned classification.

2014	Members (Q4 2014)	Growth in Members	Growth in Active Users	Alexa Internet Rank
Facebook	1,440 m	1 %	- 9 %	2
Twitter	300 m	10 %	7 %	8
Instagram	300 m	32 %	47 %	26

Figure 2: Relative and absolute growth of members/users in own illustration
(Alexa, 2015, GWI, 2014)

Two papers shall especially be highlighted at this point to reflect the current state of knowledge in regards to account value in social networks.

First of all, the publication of Schreiner and Hess (2013a), which can be seen as the staring point of the dissertation, successfully applied the van Westerndorp's Price Sensitivity Meter (PSM) (1976) to investigate the willingness of Google Plus and Facebook users to pay for privacy-enhancing additional features. The research aim was to statistically examine whether a so-called Freemium model, an omnipresent pricing structure in online businesses that consists of a free and a premium version, could be applied to the two social networks. Thereby, the paper serves as a perfect example of accurate data collection through online surveys and application of a recognised and advanced technique to estimate willingness to pay. Despite the recognition of the well-outlined and integrated PSM method, it must be emphasised that the chosen approach is considered to be lacking incentive compatibility by state of the art literature (Kim et al., 2012, Miller and Hofstetter, 2009). Beyond the lack of theoretical grounding, the PSM mechanism is rather difficult to explain and to illustrate in graphs. Another weakness of this paper is the relatively small sample size of 160 participants and non-representativeness concerning age and educational background (primarily students), which further limits the possibility to draw general implications. Those weaknesses, especially in regard to the used mechanism, directly impact the dissertation as they provide profound insight into the major difficulties in identifying consumer's monetary preferences, as they usually don't want to disclose it (Wertenbroch and Skiera, 2002).

Secondly, the paper of Bauer et al. (2012), which explores the perceived value of actively as well as passively uploaded information on the social networking platform Facebook, is of utmost importance. In the course of their study, the authors tested several variations of the Becker-DeGroot-Marschak mechanism on a large sample of 1045 participants in form of an online survey-based experiment. However, a serious weakness of the study is the distorting influence of external stimuli (e.g. free iPhones), which had a significant correlation with the stated WTP (Bauer et al., 2012). In other words, the WTP was fluctuating depending on whether a low- or high-value external incentive was used. Moreover, the study is completely lacking a control group in order to make statistical adjustments[2] retrospectively. As a result, the authors regression model to identify driving factors for participants WTP only has a "small explanatory value of 14.5%" and consequently "couldn't explain one's profile valuation" (Bauer et al., 2012, p. 8)

In the further evaluation, the study outcomes are mainly transferred to the context of online privacy by the authors, but are also dependent on the perceived value of the overall online profile (WTA of the profile subtracted by the social surplus), which is one of the research questions of my dissertation.

$$\sum_{k=1}^{n} perceived\ Risks \times Value\ of\ the\ Profile = WTP\ for\ privacy$$

Interrelation under the assumptions of rationality[3] (own illustration calculated according to (Neus, 2013)):

2.2   Characteristics of Network Industries

In order to appropriately analyse the value of an Instagram account in later steps, the social network Instagram has to be set into the right context. This guarantees correct assessment of the special environmental circumstances in a network industry, where the focus shifts from valuing an entity instead of valuing its connection to other entities.

Characteristics of NI:	Instagram
Network Effects (direct)	Within user base
Complementarity and Standards	Smartphones and PCs
Economies of Scale	Degression of fixed costs since launch
Switching Costs and Lock-In	Disabled transfer of information to other platforms

Figure 3: Characteristics of Network Industries applied to Instagram (own illustration)

---

[2] Concerning the distorting influence of external stimuli on the stated WTP

[3] Formula demonstrates the connection between the study of Bauer et al. and my research question.

Figure 3 analyses the social network with respect to the dominant theoretical frameworks of network industries by using four characteristics that distinguish those industries from ordinary markets for commodities or stocks (Gabel, 1994, Majumdar and Venkataraman, 1998, Shy, 2001). The first and eponymous factors in such industries are *direct and indirect network effects*, which may also be regarded as positive externalities (Akerlof and Kranton, 2000, Katz and Shapiro, 1986). In the case of Instagram, direct networks (within one side) are present between users of the platform. Moreover, they can also be seen as the driving force that enabled Instagram to quickly establish a critical mass of users (tipping point), where the process of gaining new users becomes self-sustaining, with no marketing costs or other incentives needed (Markus, 1987, Valente, 1995). A large and growing body of literature label this unique process as the "bandwagon effect" (Farrell and Saloner, 1985). Indirect network effects on the other hand, are considered to be present at a minor extent at the moment, but may rise with the gradual implementation of sponsored content in 2014 and 2015 (Instagram, 2014). However, the key problem is that it may be hard to distinguish in reality whether a network effect is truly direct or indirect since an exact demarcation between the same and a different entity or side is impossible[4].

The second characteristic focuses on (technical) *complementarity to other products or services*, which often requires a compatible standard resulting from a negative cross elasticity in demand (Kuraitis, 2009). In the case of Instagram, the application requires a smartphone or tablet with Android or iOS software to operate. Limited account management functions or non-interactive Web 1.0 viewers are available via PC.

Moreover, network industries usually face immense *economies of scale* as the set up costs (fixed costs) of a platform or software are assumed to be relatively high (Shy, 2001). Due to the fairly low distribution and maintenance costs (variable costs) in the case of electronic copies, firms in network industries have the opportunity to achieve a fast degression of fixed cost, especially after reaching a critical mass (Koshal, 1972). Instagram is no exception in regards to economies of scale and has been able to significantly reduce the cost per new user since the launch of the platform (TechCrunch, 2010).

Lastly, *switching costs and lock-in effects*, which occur if members of a platform try to switch to a similar service, are also present on Instagram (Klemperer, 1987, Kuraitis, 2009, Shy, 2001). They play a distinct role in the estimation of the value of an account, as users may value their account higher as the rebuilding of an account

---

[4] E.g. are business profiles on the same or on a different side in relation to a normal account?

may come with high or prohibitive costs. Shapiro and Varian (2013) provide a holistic framework that further classifies various sources of lock in effects. In the case of Instagram contractual-, information-, search- and especially data conversion costs should be emphasised at this point. Shapiro and Varian (2013) didn't consider the huge potential losses of connections in the network through switching (e.g. followers, followings, comments and likes), which might exceed the pure data transfer costs by far.

All in all, the investigated pivotal characteristics of network industries can easily be transferred to the social network Instagram. Hence, the above mentioned, underlying theoretical models have to be taken into account in the methodology of the empirical research. Questions have therefore been specifically designed to not only survey the value of an account but also to reflect direct network effects that enable the emergence of it. However, it still has to be emphasised that Shy's (2001) framework of characteristics only reflects a small piece of digital reality and strategically marginalises mixed forms of industries.

2.3 The Social Network Instagram

2.3.1 Historic Development

After describing Instagram in the right business context, this section now targets the social network itself from a microeconomic point of view, which enables a better understanding of the following chapters.

Instagram was developed by Kevin Systrom und Mike Krieger after working on their HTML5-based check-in software burbn, which combines elements of Foursquare and Mafia Wars (Systrom, 2010). The extended version of burbn, which allowed users to share, comment and like pictures was initially released on Apple's App Store on October 6th 2010 (Desreumaux, 2014). At the same time, the project was renamed to Instagram, which is a portmanteau of "telegram" and "instant camera" and according to the developers "better captured what you were doing" in the application (Systrom, 2010). Their funding in the development phase from the 5th of March 2010 onwards, raised a total amount of 500.000 USD, including early, well-known internet-investors such as Andreessen Horowitz and Twitter co-founder Jack Dorsey (Siegler, 2010). From a computer science point of view mainly open source solutions were used such as Ubuntu Linux, nginx-webserver, Django and PostgreSQL. Similar to Foursquare and Dropbox, Instagram is hosted in an Amazon EC2 cloud, which helped to reduce infrastructure and maintenance costs through economies of scale (Bains, 2014, Armbrust et al., 2010).

In early 2011, the development team decided to integrate a "hashtag" function, which is a method for content based filtering for microblogging services and social networks. Although, hashtags were mainly used inside the boundaries of twitter[5] at that point in time, they rapidly set out to be a useful tool to find photos with a specific theme or content on Instagram. On the 3rd of April 2012 Instagram launched their services for Android based operating systems, which drastically increased global dissemination at that time (Thomas, 2012). A version for personal computers is not in the interest of the company and many key features are still only available via mobile devices.

The same month, Facebook announced to take over the 13 employee strong Instagram team for the price of one billion US dollars, which was equal to 1,592 billion British pounds in 2012, in cash and stock and ranks at the highest takeover price in the industry (Figure 4) (Facebook, 2012). After the deal was closed and approved by the Federal Trade Commission in the U.S. in September 2012, Facebook decided to keep the company independently managed. However, Facebook has a decisive influence on the company in relation to the monetisation of its business model and launch of advertising services (Instagram, 2015a).

Digital Photo Service	Overtaking Firm	Price in USD	Year
Picasa	Google Inc.	5 million	2004
Flickr	Yahoo	30 million	2005
Photobucket	News Corporation	300 million	2007
Instagram	Facebook Inc.	1.000 million	2012

Figure 4: Comparison of takeover prices within the industry (own illustration)

2.3.2 Distinct Features

As established before, Instagram successfully convinced consumers since its launch on October 6th 2010 to adopt their new social networking platform. The creators Kevin Systrom and Mike Krieger base their success on several key components.

One component was the strict implementation of a differentiation strategy, which aimed to separate the network from their main rival at that time, Facebook. This was mainly achieved through limiting the potential photo size to a square shape, similar to Kodak Instamatic and Polaroid images, which improved clarity, simplicity and mobile accessibility (standard scripts of transfer and substantially lower traffic of data).

---

[5] Hashtags originated in twitter in 2007

Moreover, Instagram enables instant photo/video upload and editing by using 24 unique and patented filters. For the first time an online service made professional photo adjustments options available for smartphones and tablets, which are otherwise only available via desktop computers (e.g. Dodge and Burn technique). Likewise, the network also served as a useful add on for Twitter, which already featured 54 million active users in Q4 2010 (Statista, 2015c). This is mainly due to the fact that Twitter did not feature an appropriate option to upload or rather edit photos from mobile devices before sharing. For this reason, Instagram mainly served as an intermediate between mobile devices and Twitter in the start up phase of the network by substantially lowering transfer costs of consumers (Manning et al., 1995). This opportunity of convincing Twitter users to sign up for Instagram was strategically used by the creators to overcome potential problems in the decisive early diffusion process of the network (Rogers, 2010, Kwak et al., 2010, Valente, 1995, Valente, 1996). Consequently, from the start up of the network, photos could be shared parallel on other social networks with a single click (Instagram, 2015c). However, Twitter realised the on-going cannibalisation and outmatch of Instagram in terms of growth rates and advised it's high-profile users (e.g. celebrities) to stop sharing Instagram links and photos on Twitter (Fiegerman, 2015).

Further, the service is still available for free, making full use of the bandwagon effect (increasing preference for a commodity due to direct network effects) and network industry theory concerning consumer's adoption of new technologies. As a consequence, the network did not have any significant source of income until early 2015, when their advertising program was launched in the US (eMarketer, 2015). This program is estimated to generate 0.59 billion in 2015, 1.48 billion in 2016 and 2.81 billion USD in 2017, due to new advertisement products for capital-intensive as well as –extensive advertisers, including the "Custom Audience" feature, which aims to reduce scattering losses (Acar et al., 2015, eMarketer, 2015, Paul et al., 2015). Other e-commerce pricing strategies to further increase sales are still feasible and may work alongside Instagram's advertising program (Lee, 2001, Turban et al., 2015). Similar to the video game market, a free-to-play pricing strategy, based on the Freemium software model, can be considered as suitable, as the incentive to join the platform remains high (Hanner and Zarnekow, 2015, Alha et al., 2014). A possible implementation of this pricing strategy for Instagram will be discussed in Section 2.5.2 alongside with a feasibility analysis. Moreover, the outcome of this study is expected to directly influence the applicability of a Freemium model.

In contrast to free-to-play pricing, pay-to-play in general is not a suitable option for social networks, aiming for a high amount of users in order to establish direct network effects (Nojima, 2007). A large body of literature investigated the negative correlation between high upfront fixed costs and speed of adoption (Barron and Torero, 2015, Ma et al., 2015, Shriver, 2015). Similarly, a part of existing users may not be willing to pay for a service, which was previously for free.

2.4 User based advertising on Instagram

Instagram is increasingly described as a microblogging platform, which enables up-load of user-generated content in smaller amount or file size than a normal blog (Culloty, Leadbeater, Zappavigna and Zhao). The uploaded content itself are usually named microposts and consist of short sentences, individual images, or video links (Aichner and Jacob, 2015). As the similarity in the name microblog and blog would already suggest, the associated revenue models are largely congruent, with the exception for revenue stemming from platform unique advertisement like Google Adsense, banner advertisements or pop-ups (Lee et al., 2015).

Users or microbloggers on Instagram generally have the opportunity to receive two types of capital-forming payments from advertising companies. One is actual monetary compensation in advance in exchange for favourable mentions of the respective brand in hashtags and pictures in line with the company´s marketing communication strategies among the users target group. In the second option users "only" receive free items or gifts from their clients in return for their microblogs. It is often, however, a mixture of both forms of compensation. Increasingly free products are also sent to Instagram users with a big audience without prior contractual agreement on advertisement, in the hopeful prospect that the recipient likes the respective products and thus discreetly advertises over a shared picture. Bloggers and companies alike embed Instagram as an integral part of their multichannel marketing campaigns amongst platforms like Twitter and Facebook for either self-promotion or to increase product sales or to enhance their brand reputation as an approachable and interactive brand.

To determine the actual value and price of this form of picture based advertising and to define the business foundation of digital social influence it is necessary to systematically examine the underlying variables of the account. It is to assume that number of followers, as user who can share, like and comment on the picture, and thus determine the outreach of a profile, is the most critical determinant in this case. Still further interaction indicators and ratios, need to be taken into account to establish the value more accurately and determine profiles that may boast a large following, but score low on interaction (e.g. over bought, inactive followers).

2.5 Significance of the study for professional practice

In general, four different stakeholders are involved in the social network, whereby three of them (Instagram users, Instagram and insurance companies) could directly benefit from the results of the study and the outcomes of the three research objectives. The fourth stakeholder, companies that seek advertising space and sponsoring partners on the platform are not targeted by this study. Though, important findings may also be derived from this empirical research as firms may achieve a better understanding of their contractual partners, especially their demographics. The advertising business model of companies is, however, widely regarded as analogous to the ones offered on Facebook.

2.5.1 For Instagram Users

As outlined in Section 2.4, ordinary people enjoy the progressively decreasing start up costs for building up a business using Instagram. However, the price of their main source of revenue is still hard to assess for individuals. While some Instagram users demand only a couple of pounds, others sell their advertising space in the form of sponsored posts for thousands of pounds per photo. For instance, Danielle Bernstein of the Blog "We Wore What " states to earn from 5,000 USD (£3,255) to 15,000 USD (£9,767) per sponsored post on her Instagram Account "@weworewhat", monetising her audience of around 1 million followers (Kapadia, 2015). This uncertainty concerning the pricing of brand partnerships may be based on three key factors.

Firstly, information about pricing of other Instagram users is scarcely available online and outside the two partners of a market transaction. Likewise, it may not be in the interest of one transaction partner to provide full information to the other party (Ballwieser et al., 2012). This form of market failure, falls in line with classical microeconomic and macroeconomic theory and results in a large amount of uncertainty in the market for sponsored posts concerning pricing as well as the quality of the service (Ottum and Moore, 1997). As a result of asymmetrically distributed information, the supply side of a market transaction faces an incentive to offer low quality sponsored posts. However, rational advertising firms take this into consideration and prefer sponsored posts with moderate or low quality due to risk aversion. In line with Akerlof's theory of 1970, this ultimately leads to an equilibrium where mainly low quality services are traded in the market (assumptions of the theory are reviewed in Appendix 1). Namely, distribution platforms such as "buysellshoutouts.com" and igshoutouts.com are affected and offer advertising space on inactive accounts. However, critics of the model stem from fact that buyers can frequently seek ways to prove the quality (e.g. by pre-testing, online user reviews or indicators for account interactiveness).

Secondly, there is no consensus on which key figures of an Instagram account are pivotal for its value, as no study previously investigated this topic. However, because the visible and predictable indicators of accounts are finite, they can be shortlisted and tested for correlation with the overall value. Hence, it enables Instagram to improve the relevant components, which increase the attractiveness of the profile for sponsored posts and brand partnerships.

Lastly, many individuals, especially beginners, in the online advertising business are not aware that the sale of advertising space also leads to variable costs for the individual user. Every single post of sponsored content may reduce the number of followers and thus one of the key figures of an account. This may on the one hand be due to a deviation in content of sponsored posts, no longer matching the interest of the person following or on the other hand due to increased post frequency, now annoying their followers. According to observation and empirical documentation the loss in the amount of followers per sponsored post varies between 0.01% and 0.8% (Appendix 2). With the help of the overall account value (WTA) and the correlation in relation to the number of followers, the optimal price could be determined at which sponsored posts should be offered (Figure 5). However, users may aim for a price that exceeds the monetary compensation, due to volatility effects that requires a risk premium[6] (RP) (Cunningham et al., 2005). Two examples, including the special scenario, where the user increases the expected number of followers through selling sponsored posts (e.g through increased reputation) are outlined in the Appendix 3. Moreover, they show that, irrespective of the assumptions, a universally valid result with the correct mathematical sign is generated by the formula.

$$p^{*}(i) = \left(\frac{-(E(\Delta N_F))}{N_F} \times r_{N_F;WTA} \times WTA \right) + RP$$

Figure 5: Formula to determine the optimal price for sponsored content (own illustration)

---

[6] Assumption: Instagram Users are risk-averse $E(u(w)) < u(E(w))$

All in all, advertising on Instagram should be viewed as a method of monetisation or gradual sale of the respective audience. In order to determine the optimal price (p*) for sponsored content, it is crucial to know the overall value of the profile (WTA) and to the correlation with the number of followers ($r_{NF;WTA}$). Both variables are part of this work and had direct impact on the selection of the three research objectives. Moreover, all variables in the formula are easy to obtain or to appreciate, and thus it offers an easy way the approximate the optimal price, using the overall account value.

2.5.2   For Instagram in Terms of a Freemium Model

As mentioned in Section 2.3.2, a Freemium model could complement Instagram's current pricing strategy and could provide additional features for a particular group of users. Thereby, Freemium is a portmanteau and describes a combination of a free (eng. Free) and a paid premium offering, which is widely used by software firms and service providers in the Web 2.0 era (Bekkelund, 2011). For instance, in-application purchases of Freemium applications resemble about 92% of revenues on Apple's App Store (Schoger, 2013). They key concept was first characterised by venture capitalist Wilson on his personal online blog in 2006, as a hybrid business model, which offers basic function for free and offers users the possibility to sub-scribe a premium version (Wilson, 2006). In the course of this, the standard version does not usually contribute to the revenue of the company (Wilson, 2006, Lee et al., 2013). However, as already emphasised, the launch of a premium version is not ex-pected to hinder the parallel expansion of Instagram's ad program.

It is of vital importance to assess, which differentiation strategy is the most appropri-ate in terms of expected revenue and applicability for the social network. Puyol (2010) identified three independent, object related possibilities (by quantity, feature, or distribution) that enable premium services to increase the derived utility of a sub-set of users. Particularly, a premium version that enhances privacy and security of user profiles in the shape of a value-added service, could be a promising approach, as various studies find a existing market among users (Bauer et al., 2012, Schreiner and Hess, 2013b, Schreiner and Hess, 2015). The practical implementation could then be composed in the form of back-up solutions, geographically secured pass-words and extended privacy settings. According to Puyol (2010) this form of differ-entiation would be assigned by feature. Similarly, other authors describe the busi-ness model as a performance-related price differentiation with self-selection (Simon and Fassnacht, 2008). Thereby, the allocation to the premium version is not manda-tory for certain individuals (Skiera, 1999). Rather, every individual assigns himself or herself, based on his individual preference, to a service (free or premium version) that maximises the respective personal utility (Skiera, 1999).

Recent evidence indicates three basic prerequisites for successful implementation of a Freemium model, which shall be analysed in the following for Instagram (Bekkelund, 2011).

In the first place, the company should hold the ability to offer its service at low variable costs, at least on the free version (Bekkelund, 2011). In the case of Instagram as a business in the e-commerce sector, high fixed costs and low variable costs, amounting to one USD per additional user can be assumed (Leber, 2012, Stähler, 2002). Furthermore, a large, established audience is necessary for advertisement for the premium version, which is present in the case of Instagram (300m users). Lastly, a sufficiently large proportion of the established user base should have a willingness to pay for the premium service (Anderson, 2009, Bekkelund, 2011). As a basis for this, user must assign a value to their own profile, which can be protected by enhanced security mechanisms and privacy settings. This value shall empirically be approximated in this study by using the willingness to accept to sell the respective profile (RQ2).

2.5.3 For Insurances

A potentially high perceived and actual value (RQ2) could open up new target groups for insurance companies. Especially, since some users generate significant revenues through Instagram as a part time job or sometimes even as a profession (analogous section 2.4). At the same time, users increasingly consider who may have access to personal data and how data is used (Dinev and Hart, 2006, Taddicken, 2014, Tucker, 2014). This form of privacy concern, can be subdivided, according to Smith et al. (1996) into four dimensions ("Collection, Errors, Secondary Use and Unauthorised Access to Information"). In particular degree, Errors and Secondary Use shall be emphasised, as they may lead to deletion of the profile and thus of the potential revenue stream.

The survey in this thesis is therefore designed to collect the main figures that could help insurances to enlarge their on-going expansion in the e-commerce sector by covering Instagram accounts (Gordon et al., 2003, Vaidyanathan and Devaraj, 2003). According to current information (August 2015) no English or German insurance company provides aforethought insurance for Instagram accounts, although a significant amount of users earn money using them. After an initial offering of account insurances, the insured sum could be based on key performance indicators, a desired sum could (for example, the WTA) or be based on the perpetuity of account revenues (Dufresne, 1990).

In summary, as a result of the existing gap in the market the expansion of digital business models, it is only a matter of time until account values have to be covered by insurance companies. Hence, the author and a team of two students are cooperating with the entrepreneurship centre at the LMU Munich for further assistance and development of a business plan, following on from this dissertation.

2.6 Conceptual Framework

2.6.1 Willingness to Accept

In the context of quantifying the personal value of an account, the distinction between willingness to pay (WTP) and willingness to accept (WTA) is of great significance for the outcome and is consequently highlighted in the conceptual framework of the study (Horowitz and McConnell, 2002). Thereby, the WTA corresponds to the monetary equivalent at which an individual is indifferent between keeping a good and abandoning it (Zeiler and Plott, 2004). On the other hand, WTP, is usually described as the maximum amount, an individual is willing to pay in order to transfer a good into his own possession. Research findings regarding the amount of the WTA have remained unchanged for the past 15 years and are aptly described by John K. Horowitz et al. (2000, p. 1): "Previous authors have shown that WTA is usually substantially larger than WTP, and almost all have remarked that the WTP/WTA ratio is much higher than their economic intuition would predict." The difference between the two metrics is partially explained by the endowment effect[7], a psychological effect that leads to higher perceived value of goods in own possession (Knetsch et al., 2001, Kahneman et al., 1991, Zeiler and Plott, 2004). Other researchers, especially in the online context, use Akerlof's (1970) assumptions regarding quality uncertainties in order to explain the discrepancy (Horowitz and McConnell, 2000, Neus, 2007, Pae, 2005). The concept refers to the uncertainty of the decision maker about the value of the commodity. Decision makers are assumed to generally avoid having to make a decision under (complete) uncertainty (Neus, 2007, Davis and Reilly, 2012, Okada, 2010). Therefore, decision makers strictly prefer to delay the purchase situation until more information about the commodity is available or expertise is gained. In the case of a decision maker not being able to defer the moment of decision to a later moment in time, he will subsequently demand for an adequate risk premium (R_f > 0) to compensate for the presence of adverse information. However, it must be

---

[7] Sometimes described as divestiture aversion

emphasised that this explanation can only account for imperfect markets, as it relies on the existence of asymmetric information.

As uncertainty is expected to play a significant role when it comes to assessing the value of an Instagram account, the used mechanism will be adjusted to mitigate a possible discrepancy (Georgantzis and Navarro-Martínez, 2010, Isik, 2004, Zhao and Kling, 2001). Current literature in the field, such as Bauer et al. (2012) often failed to consider this significant difference and consequently received distorted results.

2.6.2 The Becker-DeGroot-Marschak Mechanism

Companies, policy makers and economists are often interested to know how much a person is willing to pay for a good or service (Albrecht and Maurer, 2000). The same applies to its counterpart, the willingness to accept (Dubourg et al., 1994). In practise, however, exact approximations are difficult to obtain or result in disproportionate cost increases (Higham, 2002). The main reason for that is, that surveyed people generally face no incentive to state their true WTP/WTA (Wertenbroch and Skiera, 2002, Breidert et al., 2006). Moreover, rational people deviate from their strategy to reveal their true WTP/WTA, whenever they see the possibility to positively influence their derived, expected utility (Neus, 2007).

Current literature concerning online social media and networks found various approaches to narrow down consumer's willingness to purchase or sell items. (Schreiner and Hess, 2013b). The most effective way, regarding implementation and consumption, are direct questions (e.g. monitoring purchasing decisions) with predetermined response options (Grossklags and Acquisti, 2007). Hann and colleagues used a conjoint analysis to measure the WTP in a cost-benefit analysis (Hann et al., 2002). This approach, while enabling deep insights into different characteristics of an acquirable product, is not a suitable option in the context of Instagram. In a previous survey, in 2013 at the University of Munich, the price range for Facebook and Google Plus users was estimated by van Westendorp's Price Sensitivity Meter (Schreiner and Hess, 2013b, van Westendorp, 1976). Thereby, it is possible that the WTP was overestimated due to the choice of the mechanism. For this reason, this study will use a modified and specifically tailored form of the incentive compatible Becker-DeGroot-Marschak mechanism. Adjustments are mainly carried out to ensure the measurement of the WTA instead of the WTP, as a significant discrepancy between the two values can be assumed (analogous to section 2.6.1) (Horowitz and McConnell, 2002, Sayman and Öncüler, 2005). Moreover, it must be emphasised that the purchase decision is classified as hypothetical, which should not significantly affect the answers to the three research objectives (Carlsson and Martinsson, 2001). However, this point will be discussed in more detail in the limitations of the study (Chapter 5.2) (Hess et al., 2014).

In the BDM mechanism itself, the interviewed person (carrier of the quantitative characteristic) will be told that a computer constructs the competing bid on random basis (Becker et al., 1964). Subsequently, the participant is asked to state a bid at which he wants to sell or purchase an item (Keller et al., 1993, Shogren et al., 2001). If the bid exceeds the generated random price, the person is able to purchase the item and has to pay the random price, analogous to the "Second Price Auction" (Vickrey, 1961). If the bid falls short of the random price, no transaction is performed and the benefit of the bidder remains unchanged. Vice versa, the WTA can be modeled by the BDM mechanism in a selling process, where an agreement over the selling process is achieved in the event of an exceeding random price over the bid of the test person. To improve incentive compatibility of the mechanism, the individual should have as little clues as possible in which interval the random price could be (Hong et al., 1987, Hess et al., 2014).

2.6.2.1 Alignments

In general, the BDM mechanism is respected as a subset of the Vickrey auction (second-price auction) against an unknown player with closed bids (Noussair et al., 2004). The Vickrey-Clarke-Groves mechanism can in turn be classified as a generalisation of the Vickrey auction with multiple objects to be evaluated (Vickrey, 1961).

The mentioned interconnections with some of the most recognised mechanisms in economics contribute to the widely accepted reputation of the BDM as an incentive compatible method to measure people's WTP/WTA; notwithstanding two special, theoretical cases, in which a lack of (full) incentive compatibility has been demonstrated and mathematically proven. (Mas-Colell et al., 1995, Milgrom, 2004). Those cases include fluctuations in the monetary value of the purchased/sold item itself (namely described as uncertainty or a lottery) and non-consequent maximisation of the derived utility by the decision maker (Hong et al., 1987, Horowitz, 2006, Kaas and Ruprecht, 2006). To avoid this point of critique, the usual assumptions are extended in order to ensure the overall incentive compatibility of the analysis in later steps. However, it must be emphasised that no narrow or unrealistic limitations must be made. Moreover, studies prove that the specific means of the BDM WTP/WTA are not significantly different from the real purchase actions (Miller et al., 2011, Steiner and Hendus, 2012).

2.6.2.2 Assumptions

The first and main assumption of the BDM mechanism is rationality of the decision maker (Bohnet and Zeckhauser, 2004, Schumpeter, 1984). According to the respective axioms, every person is expected to strive for additional wealth with minimum sacrifice (Bohnet and Zeckhauser, 2004, Schumpeter, 1984). In other words, decision makers are modelled as selfish and therefore maximise the expected utility through launching an individually optimal bid (Horowitz, 2006). These assumptions concerning rationality are largely consistent with the extend model of "homo economics" in other economic- and business-related subjects (Kirchgässner, 2008).

However, the widening assumption that decisions are made solely for financial incentives is not necessary for the BDM mechanism.

Secondly, the presented formula only accounts for single item auctions (Becker and Gutsche, 2007, Berninghaus et al., 2006). Consequently, the good is characterised as homogenous and not divisible.

Thirdly, the preferences of the tenderer can be described by the von Neumann-Morgenstern utility theorem (Fishburn and Kochenberger, 1979, Von Neumann and Morgenstern, 2007).

Fourthly, it is assumed that bidder has no clue in which interval the random price is allocated.

Lastly, to ensure assumption number four and overall incentive compatibility, the test individual has to disclose its WTA at the same point in time when the computer based random prise becomes clear. Subsequently, the auction would be classified as a simultaneous auction (Noussair et al., 2004). On the one hand, early announcement of the random price could result in a deviation from the true WTA, in hope for an optimisation of the derived utility. On the other hand, late disclosure may lead to mistrust into the mechanism and the fact that the opposite bid is constructed on a random.

2.6.2.3 Inventive Compatibility

This step independently analyses, whether the selected auction mechanism is truly incentive compatibility, when being transferred to the context of the willingness to accept. Consequently, it must be demonstrated that none of the actors may benefit from unilateral deviation and therefore the mechanism leads to a situation, in which every bidder has an incentive to call his WTA (Chen and Tang, 1998, Laux, 2001).

In this particular case of the Vickrey auction, the incentive situation of the subjects is of particular importance, as the other actor (in this case, computer-controlled) only provides a random price (in the BDM case, computer-controlled) (Becker et al., 1964). Analogous to other auction mechanisms, the BDM achieves its incentive compatibility through the decoupling of the auction price and the transaction price (monetary equivalent the buyer has to pay) (Müller et al., 2009). This relationship between the auction, the transaction price and the respective benefits are shown in Figure 6. Accordingly, the derived utility of the seller (in this study: seller of the Instagram profile) depends on the expected profit (π), which can in turn be influenced by two possible events. The decision outcome is formed by the choice of the bid of the seller (B_S) as well as by the opposing state of environment, which is represented by the computer based random price (B_r). In the decision process, the seller is familiar with the emergence of B_r (random character) and is therefore unable to form expectations about its value. According to Neus (2007), the decision type would consequently be classified as "with uncertainty".

The first option is that the bid of the seller (B_S) is smaller than the random bid (B_r) and as a result the transaction of the good is carried out. In the process, the seller loses the (true) value of the good (v_S) and receives a monetary compensation (B_S). In the formula, the resulting change in the utility of the seller is quantified by the subtraction of $B_S - v_S$.

In the event that B_s is greater than B_r the utility remains unchanged.

$$u_S(\pi) = \begin{cases} B_S - v_S & \text{if} \quad B_S \leq B_r \\ \\ 0 & \text{if} \quad B_S > B_r \end{cases}$$

Figure 6: Incentive compatibility in own illustration (u = utility; π = profit; v = true WTA; B = Bid; s = Seller; r = random)

The two cases demonstrate the independence of the bid from the transaction price. Due to decoupling it is not rational for the seller of the Instagram account to deviate from a bid in the amount of the true WTA ($B_S = v_S$). As usual, when proving the incentive compatibility, the case of over- or understatement of B_S is described in the following (Rieck, 2010).

The true WTA of the seller is higher than the bid submitted ($v_s > B_S$)

In the described case, the seller understates his true willingness to accept. Thereby it is possible that random bid (B_r) is higher than the bid of the seller (B_S), but still below the true willingness to accept (v_S). As a consequence, the seller participates in a transaction, which always reduces the derived utility if B_r is strictly smaller than v_S. Such an action of the individual would be classified as irrational and is therefore violating the first assumption (Becker et al., 1964, Schumpeter, 1984).

The true WTA of the seller is smaller than the bid submitted ($v_s < B_S$)

Under this condition, the seller exaggerates B_S through a bid that is larger than its true WTA (Bauer et al.). As a result, the event that the random bid (B_r) is smaller than B_S, but still above the true WTA (Bauer et al.) becomes possible. Thereby the seller's utility remains unchanged and he is unable to internalise the positive utility ($B_r > v_S$) due to overstatement of the bid (B_S).

3 Research Methodology

3.1 Rationale

3.1.1 Research Plan

The methodology section of the dissertation can be divided into three major steps that specifically address the underlying research objectives. First of all, with the aid of the theoretical concept of WTA/WTP and taking into account the special circumstances of value creation in social networks, due to network industry characteristics, an incentive compatible method needed to be established used to investigate participants´ willingness to accept for existing Instagram accounts. The implementation of the method is, as outlined in section 2.6.2 closely related to the Becker-DeGroot-Marschak (BDM) mechanism, which achieves its widely accepted incentive compatibility through pretending an actual purchasing scenario, in combination with a random bid of the buyer (Becker et al., 1964). However, the mechanism was slightly modified in order to correctly measure the price in a sale, rather than in a purchasing scenario (Horowitz and McConnell, 2002, Sayman and Öncüler, 2005). This is due to the theoretical concepts of the WTA/WTP, which highlight a significant difference between the two variables (section 2.6.1). Finding and mathematically framing the mechanism could be seen as the most critical point of the dissertation and has profoundly contributed to state of the art research in this area. Thus the attempted solution of RQ1, has already extended current literature in order to facilitate research on point RQ2 and RQ3 through quantitative analysis following on in the next section. The mechanism to determine WTA, is then directly applied in the survey to answer the remaining research questions.

In a second step, following the deductive approach, the average willingness to accept is specified by analysing primary data and using the statistical software SPSS (IBM, 2013). The results are then graphically presented and analysed for distribution using the Kolmogorov–Smirnov test and other non-parametric tests, in the case of non-normal distribution of values.

Lastly, correlations between demographic variables, key Instagram account metrics (e.g. number of followers, average like per media) and the willingness to accept are calculated to different confidence levels by using a broad range of specifically tailored correlation coefficients.

3.1.2   Justification

The main reasons for adopting this approach are:
The choice on the implemented procedure to measure the willingness to accept (RQ1) has, as already mentioned, been taken on the basis of previous work in the same research area. After extensive literature review, the currently available research body presents us with four different theoretical approaches that were shortlisted and critically assessed for my dissertation in section 2.6.2. Hence, the incentive compatible Becker-DeGroot-Marschak mechanism will be used in the dissertation.

In regards to the approximation of the WTA (RQ2), a quantitative approach is expected to be best suited to answer the described research question. This stems from the fact that quantitative approaches in general are more cost effective for high amount of responses, often featuring a higher generalisation and may statistically identify spontaneous occurrences or biases (Zikmund et al., 2012). Moreover, quantitative research is the basis for a prediction of the WTA of non-surveyed Instagram accounts and similarly for identification of significant correlations with other measurements (RQ3) (Creswell, 2013). A qualitative approach, in contradistinction, would be advantageous to gain understanding of underlying reasons and for an in-depth analysis (Creswell, 2013). In addition to that, a qualitative approach has the edge over a quantitative one during the development process of new theories and in some areas due to its enormous flexibility (Moriarty, 2011). Obtaining secondary data is not an option, as no appropriate data set is, according to the author's knowledge, available for meta-analysis. With focus on the three different methods to collect primary data, a survey is perceived to be the right choice, as it enables to gather primary, quantitative data of a relatively large sample. Especially closed ended questions, which don't allow respondents to give answers in their own way, simplify the survey process as well as the evaluation time and coding in SPSS (Steckler et al., 1992). Consequently, the approach enables a high response rate, which could drastically affect whether alternative studies would reveal similar information (reliability). Moreover, validity, generalisability could be improved and potential forms of arising bias such as the interviewer or interviewee bias could be leveraged (Walter et al., 1998). It should also be emphasised that the requirements in terms of sample size are exceptionally high, as a high dropout rate in regards to surveyed people that are underage or don't have an Instagram account can be expected[8] (Schröder, 2014).

3.2 Operational

The author's previous experience at LMU Munich has shown that the combination of direct approaches of potential participants and the usage of social media for online questionnaires, lead to the highest sample size. Moreover, past research shows that purely online-based quantitative research are significantly more biased than combined ones (Lefever et al., 2007, Wright, 2005). As a result, a paper based version (Appendix 4) and an online version of the same questionnaire were used for data collection.

3.2.1 Survey Design

The starting point of the online as well as the paper-based questionnaire is the dichotomous question whether the individual is a registered member on Instagram (Figure 7). In the "real life version" this question will be asked orally before the test person receives the questionnaire. However, care was taken that every time an individual could not answer the questionnaire, due to a lack in affiliation in regards to the online social network, the case was recorded in order to identify an accurate diffusion rate of the sample. The online survey, which was constructed using Qualtrics (Qualtrics, 2014), automatically skips to the end of the question if an individual answers the question "Are you on Instagram?" with "No".

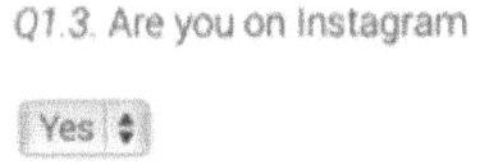

Q1.3. Are you on Instagram

Yes ⬧

Figure 7: Question 1 (own illustration)

The next block of questions, which relates to the second research objective, (RQ3) then assesses relevant demographic variables (Figure 5). Thereby, U.S. national surveys and past research in the online privacy context served as a recognised template to answer research questions (UCLA, 2015). For example, questions concerning gender, age and education were already implemented in the previous work concerning Facebook and enabled great insights in the emergence of consumer's willingness to accept. The item measuring the highest level of education is specifi-

---

[8] 19% of Germany's and UK's population are expected to be on Instagram regularly

cally tailored to the country (national designations) and is dependent on the selected country of permanent residence, which was assessed using a 195-country dropdown menu in an earlier question. As this feature is only feasible in the online questionnaire, two different paper based surveys (English and German) were constructed to assure the quality of the data (Appendix 4).

In addition to the described demographic items, marital status was included, as some profiles perceive to be trending by mentioning the marital status as "single" in their biography ("Quote Box" since 2014). Therefore, this explanatory variable will be analysed in regards to its correlation to the overall WTA as well as to a possible difference between genders. Moreover, the income range is quantified in 10,000 steps (in local currency) as past research find a significant correlation between WTA and income. (Horowitz and McConnell, 2003, Shogren et al., 1994) However, theoretical arguments, in regards to the account value of a social network, can both justify a positive as well as a negative correlation. For instance, wealthy people could easily invest money in building a new Instagram account (lower WTA) account on the one hand and on the other hand assign every possession with high value (diminishing marginal utility of money) (Joyce, 2011, von Nitzsch, 2006). In summary, however, a weak positive correlation between WTA and income can be expected in the analysis.

The third block of questions raises key account metrics of individuals to contribute to RQ3. In the course of this, all directly visible account metrics from the main Instagram profile page were included in the survey. They include, as specified in the Appendix 4, the number followers, -followings and -posted pictures (Instagram, 2015b). Moreover, additional items were carefully assessed and shortlisted by a group of six popular, German Instagram users[9]. In line with several online analytic tools, additional items were considered as useful to explain consumer's WTA to sell the respective Instagram account (Iconosquare, 2015, Simplymeasured, 2015). Namely, the estimation of the average number of likes, comments, the sign-up year and whether the test person has ever engaged in a business cooperation on Instagram (e.g. marketing, promotion of products, sponsored content,...) could have an influence on the WTA. In addition, an attempt is made to categorise Instagram accounts, which enables a broad range of implications for the dissertation as well as for future research to come. Participants can select between nine different categories covering the most prevalent hashtag groups such as beauty, fashion travel, food etc.

---

[9] Users from 1000 to 100,000 followers; Nina Stechele, Isabel Banzerus, Laurin Angermeier, Larissa Albrecht, Kimberly Schäfer, Tarek Fetih

After asking whether business collaborations have been established (Q15a), survey provider Qualtrics will automatically skip to the next relevant question depending on the answer of the respondent. In case a user has been working with brands in any form, participants will be asked whether the collaboration involved free products (Q15b) or money (Q15c) in exchange for promotional services. Only if both questions have been answered positively Q14b will allow participants to give an indication on how much revenue they gain from Instagram. Consequently, in case a user has not engaged in promotional activities Q15b, Q15c and Q14b will be omitted.

The final block of the survey aims to measure the monetary equivalent at which a person would sell the individual Instagram account (analogous to 2.4.2) in a hypothetical BDM scenario (Figure 8). Thereby, the test person is notionally introduced to the BDM scenario and thus receives support in finding the true WTA (Lusk and Shogren, 2007, Silva et al., 2007).

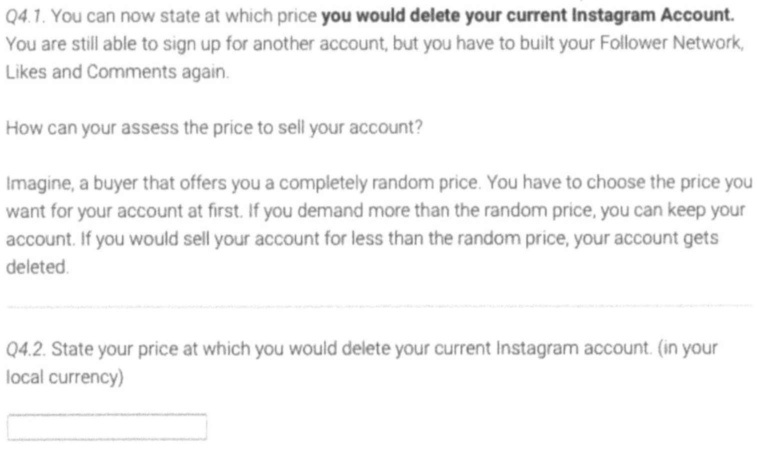

Q4.1. You can now state at which price **you would delete your current Instagram Account.** You are still able to sign up for another account, but you have to built your Follower Network, Likes and Comments again.

How can your assess the price to sell your account?

Imagine, a buyer that offers you a completely random price. You have to choose the price you want for your account at first. If you demand more than the random price, you can keep your account. If you would sell your account for less than the random price, your account gets deleted.

Q4.2. State your price at which you would delete your current Instagram account. (in your local currency)

Figure 8: Measuring Consumer's WTA (own illustration)

In addition, survey participants were able to voluntarily state their Instagram account name, for evaluating false statements in the key account metrics section of the survey (Figure 9). A review was carried out within 24 hours for each completed survey with stated account name, in order to avoid large changes of metrics, such as the number of followers, in the meantime. Subsequently, the name was, in accordance with the Ethical Guideline, promptly deleted in order to prevent possible inferences to a single person.

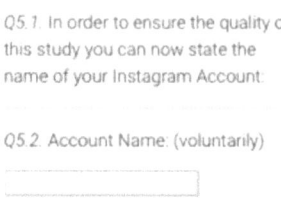

Q5.1. In order to ensure the quality of
this study you can now state the
name of your Instagram Account:

Q5.2. Account Name: (voluntarily)

Figure 9: Validation process of account performance indicators (own illustration)

3.2.2 Collection of Evidence

3.2.2.1 Location

Evidence was collected by primary research through an online as well as non-guided paper based questionnaire from June to August 2015. The target group was sought to resemble current Instagram user demographics in order to minimise the dropout percentage of users that do not have an Instagram account. The locations of the paper-based and iPad-guided survey were threefold with all locations being heavily frequented by Instagram's potential target group: First of all a large proportions of study examples were gathered on campuses (LMU Munich, TU Munich and MMU Manchester), secondly local places of interest and sights were targeted and shopping malls proved to be a popular place to find participants.

Moreover, additional responses came from several other countries outside of Germany and the UK, using the researcher's existing website and social media platforms (Facebook and Instagram). In particular, university groups on Facebook have proven to be very effective to achieve high response rates in a short amount of time. The possible occurrence of deviating results, in correlation with the research location and difference between the personal contact and online anonymity, are evaluated after the data collection. Similarly, the increased incidence of students in the sample is analysed in the following section.

3.2.2.2 Sampling technique

As the entire population of Instagram users is too large to survey, a carefully selected sample is used to represent the whole population of Instagram users. The percentage distribution of Instagram in the target area, remains unclear after extensive literature research, however, the similar distribution and size of Twitter likewise provides useful data for the social network Instagram (Spannaus, 2014). Thus, considering the overall population of each country, about 10 million Instagram users can be assumed for Germany and around 6 million for England. By exclusion of underage users (according to the ethical guideline of the university) and under normal distribution assumption, the number of possible test persons drop by an additional 40%, as already 90% of users are under 35 years (Smith, 2014). Finally, the number of potential subjects for the survey should level around 6 million for Germany and 3.6 million for England. The sample from the specified cutting of the overall population would generally be classified as probability sampling, as each member of the population features a probability of being selected larger than zero (Goodman and Kish, 1950). However, the probability of participating in the survey is not entirely equal as convenience sampling and chain referral sampling also played a role during the collection of evidence. Convenience sampling mainly occurred online in Facebook groups in order to optimise cost efficiency and to achieve a large sample size (Anderson, 2001). On the contrary, this may limit generalisability of the results to some extent, as the sample is not entirely representative for Instagram. Furthermore, systematic biases may occur, allowing theoretical results to differ from the results of the sample (Exploarable, 2009). Similarly, chain referral sampling played a role as the survey was distributed on the Authors social media platforms (Ahn et al., 2007, Biernacki and Waldorf, 1981). Friends independently shared the posted link for the online survey with others and thus created a snowball effect (exponential, discriminative snowball sampling) (Exploarable, 2009). After a few days, the survey circulated on social media platforms, probably because of interest in the topic and the relatively low average completion time of 2.5 minutes on average (analogous to section 4.1). Other reasons could stem from the fact that the online version was easy to use and almost all questions could be answered by simply pressing a button or by using a drop down menu, even on mobile devices. The distribution of responses per day on Qualtrics.com in Figure 10 further support the theory of exponential dissemination and represent a typical form for diffusion processes on social media platforms due to network effects (analogous to the snowball effect) (Katona et al., 2011, Valente, 1996). Likewise, the peak amount of completed surveys amounted to n=76 on a single day.

Figure 10: Snowball Effect of Survey Responses (own illustration)

In conclusion, the sample features many characteristics of a random probability sample, however, the large number of participants necessary in combination with budget restrictions led to some distorting effects of nonprobability sampling.

3.3 Research Problems and Actions of Mitigation

Several problems may arise throughout the research process, which may drastically influence the findings concerning the three main objectives. The biggest concern is to achieve an almost representative sample of the respective population (Instagram users as part of the population). As the second and third objective are purely based on the statistics of the primary data, the ability to draw general implications may rise and fall with the degree of all goodness criteria (objectivity, validity and reliability). Objectivity may not be a problem during the interpretation of the data (due to close ended questions) but is considered to play a significant role during the process of asking people on a one on one basis at the university. Consequently, interviewed people may be affected by the frame of the investigation and do not call their true willingness to accept, despite the incentive compatibility of the methodology used. Moreover, reliability is heavily correlated to the sample size of the study. As a result, time constraints in the process of data collection could reduce accuracy of the test and consequently the test-retest reliability (Krahnen et al., 1997). In other words, future studies could lead to divergent results, due to measuring another part of the relevant population of Instagram users. It should also be emphasised, that a single item exclusively measures the willingness to accept. Thereby, a commonly used method (several items measure WTA) to increase reliability is excluded by the lay-out of the questionnaire[10]. Validity, which is considered to be the most important criteria, may develop to be a problem in this study (Bortz and Döring, 2006). Due to second variable effects, several other independent variables could influence the measurement of the willingness to accept and distort the significance of the correlation to other variables (demographic as well as account performance indicators) in later steps. Examples of distorting variables could be a lack of comprehension of the BDM process, which could have a variety of reasons (e.g. distraction or language), the dummy variable (two distinct levels) whether uploaded photos are backed-up in a second storage or knowledge about the business opportunities that large Instagram accounts enable. Furthermore, the high percentage of students in the sample, due to online distribution in Facebook groups of universities in Germany and England as well as due to the location of the paper based survey, may significantly dis-

---

[10] A second item will drastically increase the complexity of the questionnaire and the BDM mechanism.

tort the three research objectives. This is based on the fact that students differ in their characteristics from a representative sample of Instagram users (e.g. income, age, education). Therefore, advanced statistical tools will be used in the evaluation process, which should highlight potential sources of distortion.

Secondly, a lack in understanding of the hypothetical Becker-DeGroot-Marschak (BDM) sales scenarios could lead to an understatement or exaggeration of the individual willingness to accept, at which a user sells an account. This problem mainly arises in online questionnaires, where no additional support is available to answer arising questions about the computer based random price in order to reduce external bias. For this reason, the BDM scenario is implemented alongside with a precise and meaningful description. In addition, a pre-test with a small sample was carried out in order to find the easiest description of the scenario that simultaneously guarantees a correct measurement of the WTA. It is to highlight here that despite being theoretically framed, no expert knowledge about digital business models is required to complete the study. Any confusion on interviewee side is likely to be due to the fact that only a small percentage of users have deliberately assessed the value of their profile before or thought about the potential loss of their accounts.

Prioritisation when mitigating risk:
1st Gaining a (almost) representative sample (size, validity, reliability, objectivity)
2nd Reduce the lack in understanding the hypothetical purchasing scenario

3.4 Ethical Issues

The described research project generally falls in line with the universities vision to "to behave professionally and ethically in all [its] activities" (MMU, 2015). Moreover, all types of data collection present ethical issues to an extent, yet this study will not involve the collection of highly sensitive data and will not allow drawing back conclusion to an individual (Figure 11). After a careful assessment of possible ethical issues two main areas were identified that need further strategic action.

First of all, the questions regarding marital status, likes and comments per picture can induce negative sentiment upon presentation and may lead to incorrectly filled answers or in favour of more socially accepted ones. This issue will be addressed in the form of "voluntary" fields to not further pressure participants. Although favourable from a research point of view, not all fields are mandatory to the questionnaire.

Secondly, the question of correct account names (Q15) to verify the actual sign up and usage of the platform may impose ethical concerns to some extent, yet they still do not impose ethical breaches as per point 8 outlined in the ethics guideline. To secure anonymity the account name will not be linked to gathered data for the analysis and the question will be treated as a voluntary field. Further, after successful verification, the account name will be deleted.

As a key rationale, the expected value of the survey for consumers, companies and research alike can be considered to be by far exceeding all costs such as privacy concerns association with data collection and should not be ruled out due to hypothetical ethical issues.

Manchester
Metropolitan
University

Q1.2.

Thank you for taking the time to answer this survey and enable valuable insights for my Master thesis and future publication at the Manchester Metropolitan University. Your answers will be completely anonymous and will not be passed to third parties. If you have any questions about the survey, feel free to contact me at andreas.a.banzerus@stu.mmu.ac.uk

Figure 11: Anonymity of the survey (own illustration)

4 Data Analysis

4.1 Sample Statistics

As mentioned above, 1024 test persons participated in the survey during the nine-week survey period between the 16th of June 0:00 GMT and the 16th of August 24:00 GMT. Figure 12 analyses the usability of data for the remaining two research objectives. Thereby, the dichotomous variable "user" with its two occurrences "yes" and "no" was coded as nominally scaled (Appendix 5). Five survey responses in the online survey had to be classified as missing variables (value = -1), since the survey was not completed. In comparison to empirical studies in the same field, this default rate of 0.5% can be deemed to be very low (e.g. 11% in Schreiner and Hess (2015)). Moreover, the auto detection algorithm of Qualtrics did not detect any responses that would be considered as spam.

Among the remaining 1024 participants, the majority (60.1%) of users were not registered on the social network Instagram (Mean > 1,50; Median = 2; Mode = 2). Nevertheless, 39.9% and thus 409 responses can be used to answer research question two and three. The dropout rate through non-membership is pleasantly low, showing the high suitability of the proposed sampling techniques. It can be argued here that through targeted approaches to potential user groups in social networks success rates could be heightened, as people already active in these networks were more likely to also be active on Instagram (Gondorf, 2015).

N	Valid	1024
	Missing	5
Mean		1,60
Median		2,00
Mode		2

user

		Frequency	Percent	Valid Percent	Cumulative Percent
Valid	Yes	409	39,7	39,9	39,9
	No	615	59,8	60,1	100,0
	Total	1024	99,5	100,0	
Missing	-1	5	,5		
Total		1029	100,0		

Figure 12: Variable: user – Frequencies (own illustration)

4.1.1 Demographic Variables

In a first step, the dichotomous, nominally scaled variable "sex" is analysed for Instagram users, which also allows drawing conclusions about the representativeness of the sample. Surveyees that did not feel represented by the two gender options were able to skip this question and have been assigned the missing answer value of -1. However this case did not manifest in practice. As shown in Figure 13 the number of female participants, with 316 in total and 77.3%, distinctly exceeds the number of male test persons, with 93 and 22.7%.

N	Valid	409
	Missing	0

sex

		Frequency	Percent	Valid Percent	Cumulative Percent
Valid	male	93	22,7	22,7	22,7
	female	316	77,3	77,3	100,0
	Total	409	100,0	100,0	

Figure 13: Variable: sex – Frequencies (own illustration)

In a sample ideally representing the overall population, the distribution in the sample should not significantly deviate from a discrete uniform distribution. Thereby, the expected frequency is obtained from the sample size of Instagram users (N = 409) divided by the number of cells (2 in the respective case). The chi-square test in Appendix 6, consequently shows that the gender distribution in the sample deviates significantly from the discrete uniform distribution (chi-square = 121.587; df = 1; Asymp. Sig. = 0.05). As the sample should ideally represent the population among Instagram users, and not the overall population, the outcome of this study indicates a significantly higher proportion of female Instagram users. Gondorf (2015) previously established the same phenomenon in a US American setting and found that 42% of female internet users are on Instagram and only 13% of males. This result by Gondorf (2015) can be converted so that out of 55 Instagram users 42 (76.4%) are female and 13 (23.6%) are male. Subsequently, Gondorf's data is analysed whether the gender frequencies are within the boundaries of sampling variations and if they are in line with current literature or whether this difference constitutes a real difference. The residuum in Figure 14, which is calculated by the difference between the expected and the actual values of the distribution, only levels at 3.7, despite the high sample size of N=409. Similarly, the chi-square, with the expected values 23.6%for males and 76.4% for females, validates that the sample does not

38

differ significantly from the distribution Gondorf found in 2015 (chi square = 0.183; df = 1; p > 0.05). The null hypothesis (H_0) of the distribution of analogous distribution can therefore be maintained with a failure probability of less than five percent. Consequently, the distribution can plausibly be explained by random noise and shows the same gender distribution Gondorf found in the US. Consequently, the gender distribution of the sample of can be regarded as highly representative for the following analysis.

sex

	Observed N	Expected N	Residual
male	93	96,7	-3,7
female	316	312,3	3,7
Total	409		

Test Statistics

	sex
Chi–Square	,183[a]
df	1
Asymp. Sig.	,669

Figure 14: Variable: sex – chi square test with Gondorf (2015) (own illustration)

The average age of respondents in the sample levels at 22.57 years (Figure 15). Similarly, the ascending assorted age list is divided by the value 22 into two halves (median value). The most frequent age was 20. The proximity of these two positional parameters to each other shows a large symmetry of the age distribution and the absence of a large set of outliers. The average distance of the cases around the expected value, which is statistically framed as the standard deviation, amounts to 4.484 years. The youngest Instagram user in the sample was 18 years old (younger individuals were screened) and the oldest 61 years. Accordingly, the overall age range amounts to 43 years.

age

N	Valid	409
	Missing	0
Mean		22,57
Median		22,00
Mode		20
Std. Deviation		4,484
Minimum		18
Maximum		61

Figure 15: Variable: age – descriptive statistics (own illustration)

The age pyramid in Figure 16 represents the age distribution split by gender of the 409 surveyed Instagram users. It shows a mediocre homogeneous normal distribution, which loses quality by excluding under 18 year olds. By inserting a normal distribution curve in Figure 16, it can be shown that a significant proportion of users must be less than 18 years old (empty area). Similar to previous steps, the large number of female users is striking. Graphically, the average age of men exceeds the average age of female Instagram users. Similarly, the average age of men and variance (standard deviation) exceeds the age/variance of female participants.

Overall, the age leaf for Instagram users forms a typical distribution, which further enhances the representativeness of the second and third research objective. Business Insider's intelligence report established in 2014 that 90% of Instagram's 150 million-user base at that time were under the age of 35, which is also the case in the present sample (Smith, 2014). Numerous other Internet sources show a highly similar distribution, but from a technical point of view, do not have the quality of an empirical study and were purely created for marketing purposes for advertising companies (Patterson, 2015, Statista, 2015a, Hermann, 2014).

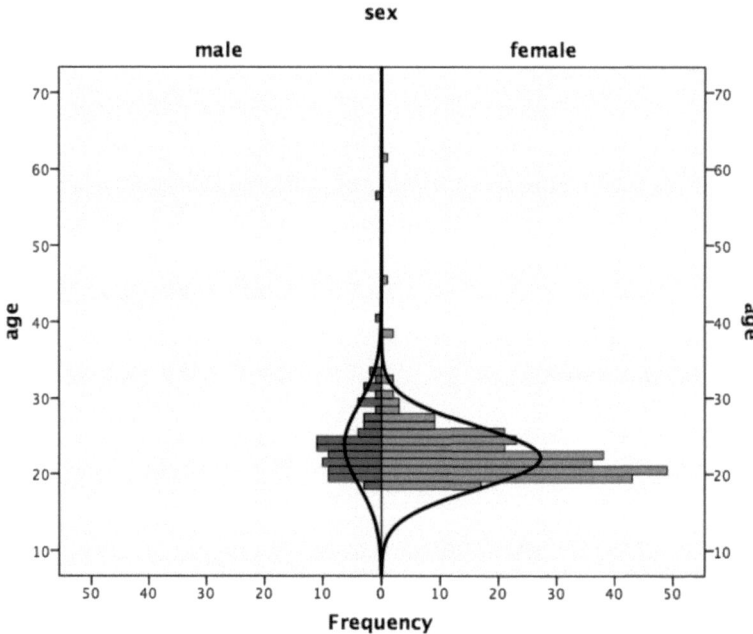

Figure 16: Age pyramid of frequencies (own illustration)

Next, the variable country displays responses from individuals with 15 different nationalities (respectively: main residences). Thereby, the vast majority of people were
German residents (356; 87%)[11]. Figure 17 also illustrates this prevailing position of
Germany in the survey in the form of a bar chart. Thereby, the abscissa represents
the 15 different countries, while the ordinate indicates the frequency. In addition, a
percentage breakdown can be found in Appendix 7. Other multiply included nationalities in the survey are Austria with 21 (5.1%), the UK with 19 (4.6%) and finally
Australia with 2 (0.5%). All in all, the study is not considered to be representative in
relation to the distribution across different countries or nationalities. Thus, possible
comparisons between countries are very limited. In addition, no overall conclusion
can be drawn regarding a percentage distribution of Instagram users across countries. Nevertheless, the participation of different countries can be seen as a positive
effect that may improve the results of RQ2 and RQ3 in terms of validity and representativeness (Rossi et al., 2013).

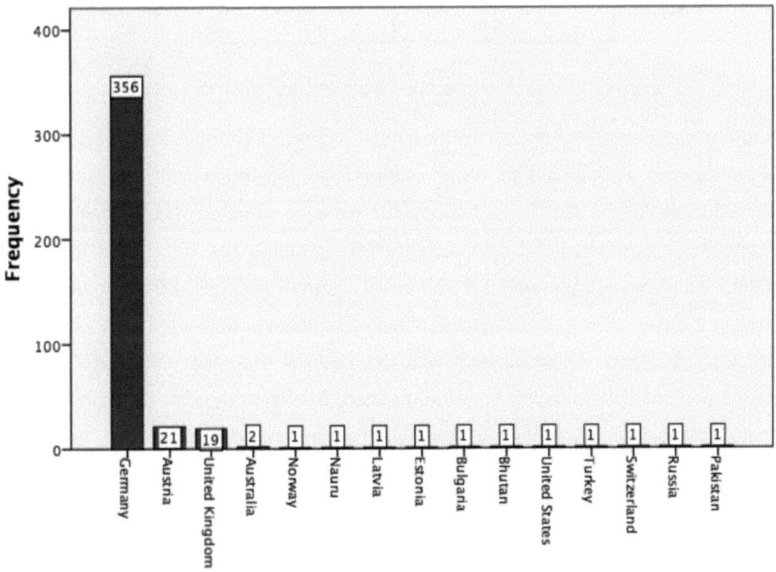

Figure 17: Variable: country – bar chart of frequencies (own illustration)

---

[11] Statistically represents the mode of the survey.

Analysing the marital status of Instagram users (Figure 18), a majority of single users becomes evident, reaching a percentage of 60.6 in the sample. Likewise, only
35.2% of respondents had a life partner when participating in the survey. The remaining 4.1% are spread over married, divorced and widowed options. This proves
that, compared to the overall population in the respective countries, which typically
consists of less of 50% singles under 30 years and about 25% singles from 30-40
years, Instagram users feature a significantly higher single-rate (Appendix 8)
(Fittkau&Maaß, 2015). An additional illustration of the distribution in the form of a bar
chart can be found in Appendix 9.

marital

		Frequency	Percent
Valid	Single	248	60,6
	Life Partner	144	35,2
	Married	14	3,4
	Divorced	1	,2
	Widowed	2	,5
	Total	409	100,0

Figure 18: Variable: marital – frequencies (own illustration)

A further demographic variable in the survey assessed the educational background
of participants. As highlighted in the methodology part, due to the non-comparable
education system in Germany, two groups were constructed. The classification in
Figure 19 is measured in 5 levels, representing mainly the UK education system
while 7 steps were constructed to represent German education. Both variables are
used in the next step to investigate a possible correlation between the WTA and the
variable education. A comparison with the Federal Statistical Office in Germany
shows a significant deviation from the standard formation ratio for Germany. In particular, the proportion of highly educated people holding a Bachelors degree or
higher is unusually high compared to the normal population (45.28% for the UK and
19.94% for Germany) (Bundesamt, 2014). Likewise, test persons holding a higher
education entrance qualification are overrepresented for Germany (67.89% compared to 28.8% on average) (Bundesamt, 2014). This may on the one hand indicate
a different educational background of Instagram users compared to the normal population or on the other hand be biased through the major number of students asked.
Moreover, the mandatory exclusion of minors leads, analogous to the previous variables, to large distortions.

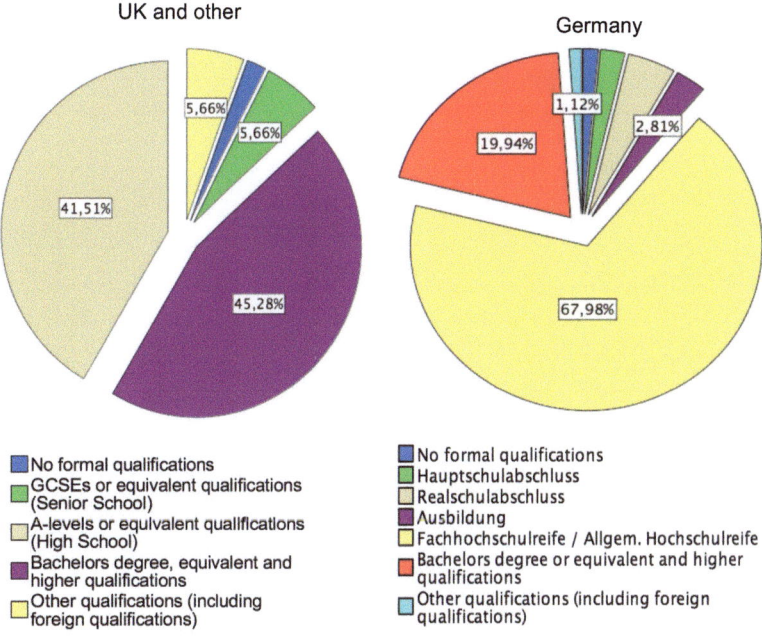

Figure 19: Variable: education – frequencies in comparison between the UK (and other) and Germany (coloration not used for comparisons) (own illustration)

Income among Instagram users may generally be considered low (dominant answer "Below 10,000" with 325 cases and 81.7%), which will be of great importance when interpreting the average willingness to accept (Figure 20). The main reason for this deviation from the normal population (average income in Germany levels around 32,000) is the previously analysed low average age of Instagram user (Statista, 2015b). An accurate determination of position parameters such as the arithmetical mean and median is not possible, since the exact gross income was not quantified by the survey, due to predominant ethical concerns. Moreover, the question was asked on a voluntary basis, which resulted in 11 missing variables out of 409 cases.

income

		Frequency	Percent	Valid Percent	Cumulative Percent
Valid	Below 10,000	325	79,5	81,7	81,7
	10,000–29,999	53	13,0	13,3	95,0
	30,000–49,999	12	2,9	3,0	98,0
	50,000–69,999	5	1,2	1,3	99,2
	Above 70,000	3	,7	,8	100,0
	Total	398	97,3	100,0	
Missing	System	11	2,7		
Total		409	100,0		

Figure 20: Variable: income – frequencies (own illustration)

Key Findings: Demographic Variables	
Variables	Key Findings
Gender	77% female users – highly representative for Inst. population
Age	Low average of 22 years, 90% under the age of 30
Country	Mainly German residents
Marital	61% single users
Education	High overall education
Income	82% below 10,000 €

Figure 21: Key Findings: Demographic Variables

4.1.2 Key Account Metrics

The analysis of the three key account metrics, which are displayed on the top of every Instagram profile, show the large heterogeneity of the sample. The range of profiles fluctuated heavily from having zero up to a maximum of 246,000 followers (Figure 22). Likewise, the high standard deviation confirms this hypothesis and reaches an average fluctuation around the 1461.21 follower high expected value of each account, of around 14,300 followers. The large deviation from the expected value of the median indicates, especially in the case of the number of followers, a highly positive skew, caused by a small number test persons with a very high number of followers (4 out of 409 people have a number of followers greater than 10.000). These so called statistical outliers have not been removed from the data set, despite exceeding the interquartile distance three times in the box-whisker plot (3×IQR) since they were not based on a measurement error but actually occurred in reality. The verification of key account metrics has been validated by manually cross checking key account metrics in 137 cases, in which surveyees have voluntarily stated their account names and ultimately showed no significant deviation from real values of their accounts.

The mean value of the 409 cases large sample in of the variables followers, followings and posts can not yet be compared to other findings as no paper empirically assessed those metrics before. However, the comparison to Facebook, where the mean number of friends is 338 and median levels at 200, shows that a right-skewed distribution is not abnormal for social networking sites. Moreover, the comparison confirms the plausibility of the results in relation to their attributes and illustrates once again the high representativeness of the gathered data set.

		followers	followings	posts
N	Valid	409	409	409
	Missing	0	0	0
Mean		1461,21	279,90	115,25
Median		121,00	147,00	40,00
Mode		50	100	0
Std. Deviation		14328,274	1158,068	270,654
Minimum		0	0	0
Maximum		246000	22265	3925

Figure 22: Variables: followers, followings, posts - frequencies (own illustration)

The average sign up year of users in the sample, which was assessed by an ordinal-scaled variable from 2015-2010 backwards, was 2013 (mean: 2.72; median: 3.00; mode: 3) (Appendix 12). The date of registration was highly significantly correlated at the level 0.01 with the total number of followers (Spearman's Correlation Coefficient = 0.356).

The following two questions, which were aiming for the average number of likes and comments play a key role when finding correlations for the WTA of the profile. The analysis shows that the average number of likes per picture levelled at 90.68 and a median of 20, whereas most of the participants received one comment per post in the past (mode value) (Appendix 13). Furthermore, both variables exhibit a high correlation at the 1% level with the number of followers, which was assessed using Spearman's rank order correlation, as the involved variables were devoid of normal distribution (Correlation: 0.765; 0,553).

The attempt to categorise Instagram accounts according to the most popular pictures themes can be deemed successful, as more than 50% of participants assigned their accounts to the labels travel and personal (Figure 23 and Appendix 14). Only technology and electronics were vaguely represented through 1,71% of accounts.

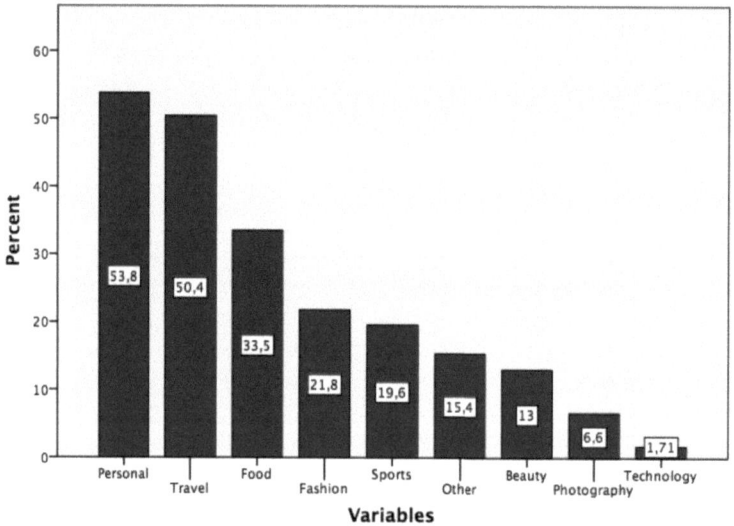

Figure 23: Variable: category – frequencies and percentage (multiple selection possible) (own illustration)

Concerning user based advertising on Instagram (section 2.4.), the statistic confirms the on-going trend of establishing an online business based on microblogging platforms. In the sample, 33 out of a total of 409 (8.1%) surveyed people have previously engaged in business cooperation, such as marketing, sponsoring or promotion), using the social network Instagram (Appendix 15). Measured against the total number of people asked (1024) the percentage still levels at 3.2%. Among the 33 microbloggers, 48.5% (16) received free products following promotional activities (Appendix 16). Furthermore, 15.2% (5) of the users stated that they have generated monetary income by using Instagram. Thereby, the average income per month levels at 315.4 Euros, whereas the median of 42 Euros shows a typical distortion of the income by a small number of high values (Figure 24). This also confirms the high span of values, ranging from 5 to 1000 euros per month, and the average distance from the expected value of 434.5 Euros. The individual values can be found in Appendix 17.

business_income

N	Valid	5
	Missing	404
Mean		315,40
Median		42,00
Std. Deviation		434,541
Range		995
Minimum		5
Maximum		1000

Figure 24: Variable: business_income – frequencies and percentage
(own illustration)

Key Findings: Account Metrics and Business	
Variables	Key Findings
Followers	121 Followers as median (1,461 as mean)
Followings	147 Followings as median (280 as mean)
Posts	40 Posts as median (115 as mean)
Since	Average sign up year was 2013
Average No. of Likes	20 likes on average
Average No. of Comments	1 comment on average
Business Activity	8.1% of users do business using their Account
Business Income	1.5% generate monthly income (315.4 € on average)

Figure 25: Key Findings – Key Findings: Account Metrics and Business

4.2 Approximation of User's WTA

4.2.1 Descriptive Statistics

For a quantification of the overall profile value, which was measured using the incentive compatible BDM method, 409 values came into consideration. Potential differences in purchasing power, stemming from values in different currencies, have been converted according to the BigMac Index to exclude any distorting currency effects in the survey (Ashenfelter and Jurajda, 2001, Ong, 1997).

A first descriptive analysis of the stated WTA failed due to a low number of potentially incorrect or insincere statement of surveyees, such as a maximum value of 10^9 (sample statistics in Appendix 18). For this reason, an exploratory data analysis was carried out using a box plot and a Stem-and-Leaf diagram in order to identify data errors and outliers (Appendix 19). In the course of this, nine possible data errors or rather outliners (value > 3×IQR) were detected. However, after checking the correlation to the number of followers in the respective cases only seven turned out to be containing erroneous values, such as a WTA of 1,000,000 at a follower count of 51. In the other two cases a WTA of 250,000 and 500,000 were stated, which is perceived to be realistic when looking at the monthly income and high number of followers (117,000 and 246,000). As a consequence, the two cases may not be removed from the sample (Bühl, 2012, Polasek, 2013). The recalculated descriptive statistics that aim to answer the second research question are illustrated in Figure 26 (Appendix 20 shows single frequencies).

Accordingly, the arithmetic mean estimates at 2,741 Euros, whereas the ascending sorted list of values is divided by the value 100 into two equal parts. The most prevalent value with 15.7 % cited by participants regarding the WTA is a price of 100 Euros in a sales scenario. The strong fluctuation of the variable, which can be derived from the high standard deviation (28,333 Euros) and the difference between the minimum (0 Euros) and the maximum value (500,000 Euros), may partly be explained using demographic and especially account metrics in the following steps of the analysis. Moreover, the distribution is skewed to the right, which is evident by the skewness greater than zero (15.727). The central moment of the fourth order, the kurtosis, indicates a heavily leptokurtic distribution. The total value of all 409 captured Instagram accounts in this survey can be estimated at 1,066,473.5 €, which is of crucial importance for both insurance companies and Instagram itself, when deciding to introduce a Freemium model.

wta

N	Valid	402
	Missing	7
Mean		2741,577
Median		100,000
Mode		100,0
Std. Deviation		28332,6586
Skewness		15,727
Std. Error of Skewness		,124
Kurtosis		260,509
Std. Error of Kurtosis		,247
Minimum		,0
Maximum		500000,0
Sum		1066473,5

Figure 26: Variable: wta – descriptive statistics (own illustration)

In a next step, the quantified WTA shall be visualised and analysed for normal distribution (Figure 27). Thereby, a logarithmic abscissa (wta_2 = log(wta)) was chosen for Figure 27 as this type of presentation enables, especially in the case of a highly positive skewness, a meaningful reflection of the total amount of cases (illustration without categorisation and logarithm in Appendix 21). Moreover, the stated WTA was classified in six ordinal-scaled categories. The ordinate shows, as usual, the relative frequency of the WTA.

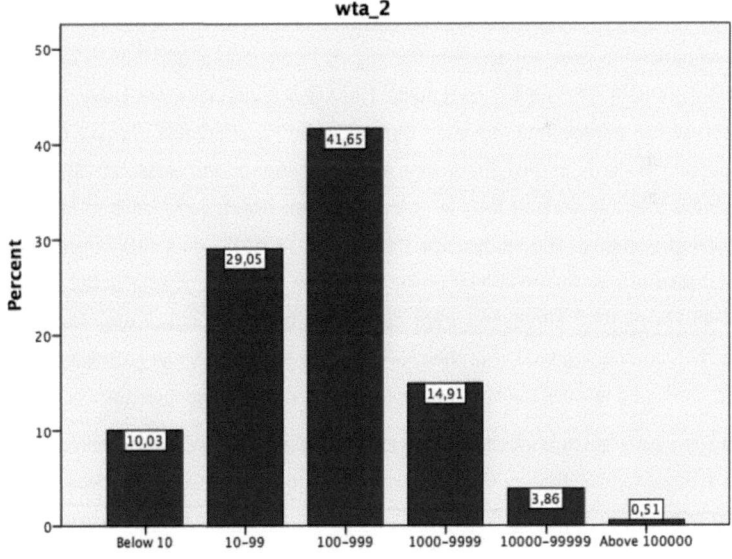

Figure 27: Variable: wta_2 – frequency (own illustration)

The bar chart in Figure 27 still forms, despite the logarithm, a soft skewness to the right in comparison to the normal distribution. Moreover, the conducted Kolmogorov Smirnov test in Figure 28, which is one of the most common and recognised methods for testing a sample for normal distribution, confirms the remaining deviation (Massey Jr, 1951). The null hypothesis (H0) of the distribution of analogous distribution to the normal distribution was consequently rejected with a failure probability of less than one percent (K-S-Z = 9.101; $p < 0.01$). For this reason, only non-parametric tests are applied in the following analysis for variables wta and wta_2.

One-Sample Kolmogorov-Smirnov Test

		wta
N		402
Normal Parameters[a,b]	Mean	2741,577
	Std. Deviation	28332,6586
Most Extreme Differences	Absolute	,461
	Positive	,428
	Negative	-,461
Kolmogorov-Smirnov Z		9,101
Asymp. Sig. (2-tailed)		,000

a. Test distribution is Normal.
b. Calculated from data.

Figure 28: Variable: wta_2 – Kolmogorov-Smirnov Test (own illustration)

In comparison to previous studies, the largely homogenous distribution of values is to highlight here. This clearly contradicts Hess and Schreiner´s pre study, where 125 of 150 (83%) participants indicated that they had no willingness to pay for privacy enhancing features in their Freemium model (Schreiner and Hess, 2015). It can be assumed that this serious fault in study has been intentionally omitted in the final, published version of the study. Also Bauer et al. (2012), who's study measured the willingness to pay for additional privacy services on social media accounts, found that 48,1% of 1045 surveyees were not willing to pay a single Euro. Their subsequently following regression of their WTP model exhibited a low R-Square value of 14.2, indicating low suitability of the model and underlying mechanism.

The superiority of the applied WTA construct applied here, achieved through a slight and elegant modification of the BDM, manifests in *better results regarding homogeneity and pricing options*. It has clearly shown that the previously chosen abstract and intangible WTP purchasing scenario of the product "privacy" lacks suitability as a survey construct, whereas the selling scenario as framed in the WTA construct was widely accepted amongst surveyees and can be held accountable for this improvement of results.

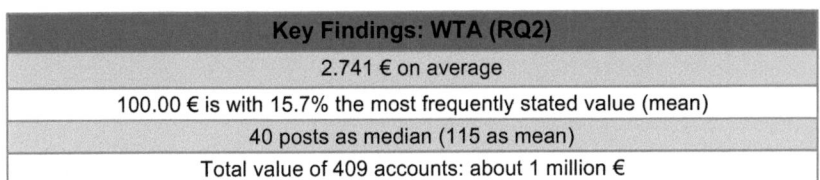

Key Findings: WTA (RQ2)
2.741 € on average
100.00 € is with 15.7% the most frequently stated value (mean)
40 posts as median (115 as mean)
Total value of 409 accounts: about 1 million €

Figure 29: Key Findings: WTA

4.2.2 Correlations with Socio-demographic Variables

In order to fully capture research question number three, the previously calculated WTA will be analysed in special regards to correlations with demographic variables as well as key account metrics in the next section. The product-moment correlation index, established by Pearson, can only be used for scale measured variables such as the WTA and the age of participants (Toutenburg and Heumann, 2008). Figure 30 consequently analyses the correlation coefficient according to Spearman and Kendall for the ordinal and nominal scaled variables such as sex, country, marital, education and income (analogous variable description in Appendix 5). The interpretation of the figures, calculated by SPSS, shows no significant linear correlation of values in the two dimensional space of the WTA and age of test persons, as the significance levels at 0.745 (Figure 30).

		wta
age	Pearson Correlation	-,017
	Sig. (2-tailed)	,745
	N	402

Figure 30: Variable: wta– Pearson correlation with age (own illustration)

However, the interpretation of Spearman's rho reveals evidence for a significant correlation ($p < 0.05$) of the annual income and the stated WTA of 0.118 (Figure 31). As Spearman's coefficient ranges from -1 to 1 the value should be interpreted as a weak positive correlation. Similarly, to Spearman's results, the conducted rank correlation coefficient test after Kendall (1938), which offers advantages in the case of outliers, amounts to 0.098 and shows a significance to the five percent level.

			wta
Spearman's rho	sex	Correlation Coefficient	,050
		Sig. (2-tailed)	,327
		N	389
	country	Correlation Coefficient	-,016
		Sig. (2-tailed)	,746
		N	389
	marital	Correlation Coefficient	,009
		Sig. (2-tailed)	,859
		N	389
	education_uk	Correlation Coefficient	-,015
		Sig. (2-tailed)	,917
		N	48
	education_ger	Correlation Coefficient	,028
		Sig. (2-tailed)	,610
		N	341
	income	Correlation Coefficient	,118
		Sig. (2-tailed)	,022
		N	379

Figure 31: Variable: wta – Spearman correlations with demographic variables (own illustration)

Overall, the value of Instagram profiles is only correlated with the annual income of users. Thus the findings are consistent with Hess and Schreiner´s (2015) and Bauer et al. (2012), who couldn't find significant correlations in regards to demographic variables. However, they both omitted a potential income influence on purchasing or sales decisions, so this study can actively contribute to enhancing their findings.

Key Findings: Demographic Correlations (RQ3)
Income has a significant correlation with WTA of 0.118
Country, education and marital are not correlated with the WTA
Women feature a higher WTA on average but difference is not significant

Figure 32: Key Findings: Demographic Correlations

4.2.3   Correlations with Key Account Metrics

The correlation of the willingness to accept with key account metrics is of particularly high importance, since strong relations would enable an estimation of the overall value of the profile, using existing and displayed account metrics. The calculation of the scale-measured items was, as required, performed using Pearson's correlation coefficient. The analysis of Figure 33 manifests that both the number of followers and the number of posts are highly significantly correlated with the overall value (p-value < 0.01). Thereby, the calculated coefficient levelled at a very high figure of 0.995 for the number of followers and for the number of posts at a relatively low figure. The number of followings, however, has no significant influence on the WTA of Instagram users.

		wta
followers	Pearson Correlation	,995
	Sig. (2-tailed)	,000
	N	402
followings	Pearson Correlation	,023
	Sig. (2-tailed)	,653
	N	402
posts	Pearson Correlation	,292
	Sig. (2-tailed)	,000
	N	402

Figure 33: Variable: wta– Pearson correlation with follower, followings and posts (own illustration)

In regards to the ordinal and nominal measured variables, highly significant correlations to the 1 percent level were found for all three. Consequently, older Instagram accounts generally feature a significantly higher personal value. Thereby, the correlation coefficient amounts to 0.221 for the Spearman coefficient (Figure 34) and 0.166 for Kendall's coefficient in Appendix 23. The average number of likes and comments has a similarly high correlation, and were both equally coefficient revised downwards by Kendall's coefficient.

			wta
Spearman's rho	since	Correlation Coefficient	,217
		Sig. (2-tailed)	,000
		N	402
	likes_avg	Correlation Coefficient	,211
		Sig. (2-tailed)	,000
		N	402
	comments_avg	Correlation Coefficient	,242
		Sig. (2-tailed)	,000
		N	402

Figure 34: Variable: wta – Spearman correlations with account metrics (own illustration)

While the established categories of Instagram accounts (such as sports related, travel-related) have no influence on the quantified WTA, the decision to do business using the social media platform has a significant one (p-value < 0.05). In other words, users with high profile values recognised the opportunity and started to sell advertising space by using sponsored posts. However, the coefficient only amounted to 0.127 for Spearman and 0.107 for Kendall, which could be the result of he relatively low number of people doing business on Instagram in comparison to the overall number of accounts (in the sample 33 out of 409 cases) (Appendix 24).

Key Findings: Account Metrics Correlations (RQ3)
High and significant correlation between the number of followers and WTA (0.995)
Low and significant correlation with the number of posts (0.292)
No significant correlation with the number of followings or account category
Older Instagram accounts are typically assigned a higher value
The number of likes and comments are a good predictor for the overall WTA
Accounts used for business purposes on Instagram generally have a higher value
The average income of people using Instagram for business levels at 315 €

Figure 35: Key Findings: Account Metrics Correlations

In summary it can be noted that the number of followers is the strongest predictor for the WTA for existing Instagram accounts. The correlation coefficient is considered to be very high, despite the large variation in the profile value. With the aid of a regression, with the dependent variable WTA and the number of followers as the independent variable, the value of an account can be determent simply by having knowledge about the total number of followers (Figure 36).

Dependent Variable: wta

		Model Summary				Parameter Estimates	
Equation	R Square	F	df1	df2	Sig.	Constant	b1
Linear	,991	41485,353	1	387	,000	168,235	2,042

The independent variable is followers.

Figure 36: Regression analysis (own illustration)

Figure 37 further pictures the result of the linear regression, which was created by the method of least squares (OLS method). Thereby, the independent variable, the number of followers, is represented by the abscissa and the ordinate shows the corresponding WTA. The model exhibits that an account with no followers (N_0) still pos-

54

sesses an average WTA of approximately 168 €. Moreover, the WTA increases by approximately 2 € with every follower on the respective Instagram account. However, analogous to section 2.6.1, it has to be emphasised that an exaggeration through the endowment effect is conceivable. Especially, a high proportion of the relatively high value for an account with zero followers (N_0) of about 168 € could be attributable to the endowment effect, as the resign-up process and reconfiguration (finding friends, settings and the resulting opportunity costs) of a new account doesn't add up to that amount.

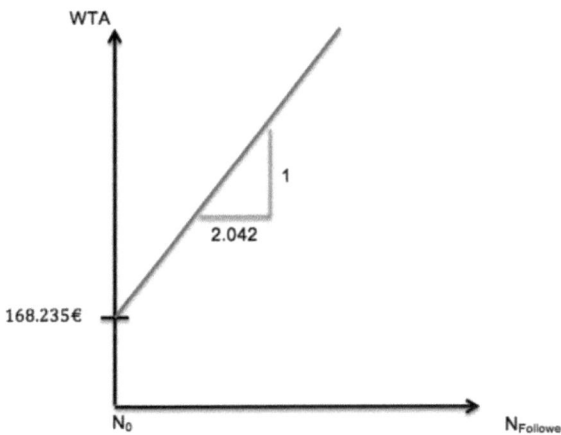

Figure 37: Linear Regression Graph (own illustration)

5 Conclusion

5.1 Implications

5.1.1 For Instagram Users

Theoretical and analytical findings in this dissertation hold high implications for Instagram users, as a continuously growing community of likeminded micro entrepreneurs. Especially people with high annual income showed high WTA values, with 33 of 409 participants even using the accounts as a form of revenue. As outlined in the introduction, these users face uncertainty and problems when pricing advertisement or so called "shoutouts", a form of reciprocal advertising. Using the theoretically introduced formula in section 2.5.1 the optimum price (p*) for sponsored posts can now easily be determined by estimating the resulting change in the overall value (WTA) by using the expected loss or increase of followers (Figure 38). The missing value for the correlation between the number of followers and the WTA was quantified as 0.995 in the analysis. For estimating the value of the individual WTA of users, the incentive compatible BDM mechanism of the survey may be used as well as the rule of thumb resulting from the regression analysis. Accordingly, the WTA amounts to 170€ plus two times the number of followers.

$$p^*(i) \quad = \quad (\frac{-(E(\Delta N_F))}{N_F} \times 0.995 \times WTA) + RP$$

Figure 38: Final formula to determine the optimal price (own illustration)

Moreover, fake followers can now easily be identified, by looking at the most plausible ratios of followers and interactions values such as likes per post or comments per post. Ultimately this enhancement may drastically increase market transparency in the near future, as a foundation for business opportunities and reduces price uncertainty.

5.1.2 For Advertising Companies

In addition to exhibiting positive effects for users, also digital advertising companies and marketing departments will benefit from the proposed results. Demographic findings clearly show which target groups can be specifically addressed through Instagram ad campaigns. A quote of 77.3% female participants among the community opens doors for gender based marketing activities and gender tailored content (Auster and Mansbach, 2012, Bruwer et al., 2011). Moreover, the network offers an above-average ratio, even among the same age group, of singles of 60.6%, which can similarly be a useful demographic for some companies to reduce scattering losses in marketing (e.g. dating platforms) (Perrey and Spillecke, 2013). Similarly, the classification of accounts into categories shows that especially posts about Travel (50.4%), Food (33.5%) and Fashion (21.8%) are trending on the social network as a large number of users share content on the respective topics. Therefore, firms in those sectors are particularly advised to intensify social media marketing on Instagram as the viral spread of content is more likely to occur (repost likelihood) and advertising is easily disguised amongst the myriad of credible, private travel, food and fashion pictures. On the contrary, posts about electronics or technology are assumed to be less frequent, as only 1.7% of users in the sample allocated their account to these topics.

A further key benefit for companies is to realistically assess the value of their own corporate accounts as an important tool to engage with the year younger customers at an average age of 22.57 years and 90% of participants at under 30 in the study. They can also now assess the value of business partner accounts when engaging in blogger cooperations and thus offer a realistic price for advertising campaigns. As a sales policy measure, the impact of Instagram remains unclear, despite being actively engaged on Instagram, most student participants hold a rather low purchasing power of less than 10,000€ per year. It is important to advise that digital marketing companies should not overrate the impact of their campaigns as the diffusion rate of 39.9% is likely to be overrated and slightly lower in the overall population. Still, given the lack of comparable approaches or even research, this study provides valuable practical insight on potential demographics, target groups and pricing options for digital marketers, that enable them to redefine their approaches, resulting in lower campaign cost through custom audience features (Strutton et al., 2014).

5.1.3 For Instagram in Terms of a Freemium model

As pointed out before, state of the art theory raises three main requirements for the implementation of a Freemium pricing strategy for online businesses (Bekkelund, 2011). Thereby, the marginal costs close to zero and the very large and growing user base of 300 million people meet the first two of them with ease. By quantifying the WTA to 100€ on median in research question two, Instagram obtains first evidence on the personal value of accounts. In combination with growing privacy concerns on the web and especially on platforms containing personal information, a premium version with enhanced privacy features could complement Instagram's revenue model in a second pillar (Smith et al., 1996, Udo, 2001, Wang and Hajli, 2014). Practically Instagram could contain back-up solutions, geographically secured passwords and extended privacy settings. Further, detailed guideline for implementation is the task of further research.

5.1.4 For Insurances

The profound personal and sometimes subjective value of Instagram accounts could be a promising new business foundation for existing and aspiring smaller insurance companies. Thereby, the conducted empirical analysis indicates a huge potential market, as surveyed accounts featured a median WTA of 2,742.58 € on average and 100€ as median. Moreover, 4.37% of the accounts possessed a WTA of 10,000€ and above. In addition to the overall account value, an insurance of the derived monthly income stemming from Instagram business activities is perceived as necessary, which is currently not available in a reasonable form for micro- entrepreneurs (with the exception of special insurance requests celebrities enjoy). This manifests in the analysis of the gathered business variables, according to which an 8.1% of the respective 409 Instagram users are currently using their Instagram account for business activities. 19.4% of these individuals even had monetary income of 315€ per month on average.

The introduction of insurance offerings could then, as mentioned in section 2.5.3, be based on key performance indicators of the account and its correlation with the overall WTA (RQ3), a desired sum of the user equal to the individual WTA (not the average expected WTA) or reflect the missed monthly income, if an account is shut down or lost.

5.2 Limitations

To capture all aspects of this study topic it is of utmost importance to also address potential limitations, as briefly touched upon in the methodology chapter. Generally, limits manifest when weighing the potential benefits and drawbacks of all options available to address a research question. Methodically there is no single best answer to each question, however through the careful elimination of research design options we are presented with very few limitations in this area.

First of all, the sampling method and situation was not fully representative and controlled as study participants "self-selected" themselves, when following online links and agreeing to participate (Khazaal et al., 2014). Therefore, not every person had the same chance to be randomly selected to participate in a controlled manner, and it is likely that participants with a keen interest in the topic were more likely to follow the study link on social media (Atteslander, 2003, Kromrey, 2001).

Secondly, different behaviour of respondents, when either completing the paper-based or online-based questionnaire, is a thinkable influence. Yet the requirements in terms of sample size, to fulfil goodness criteria, made it necessary to use two different media. When answering a paper-based questionnaire in a public space, individuals may feel more under pressure to give socially favourable answers or were hesitant to answer questions regarding income, than when answering online questionnaires in the safety of their own homes. A further analysis between the two forms of questionnaire have not been addressed here, as in hindsight answers could not be discriminated according to time, place and medium used.

Thirdly, state of the art statistical tests such as Pearson's or the non-parametric counterpart, Spearman's rank correlation, both reveal a weakness in regards to the correlation between WTA and the number of followers. The foundation for the problem is the calculation method of both tests, which minimises squared distances to the regression line (Schmidt and Hunter, 2014). For this reason, higher values are generally more crucial in the determination of the correlation line. Ultimately, this could possibly result in an overestimation or underestimation of the correlation coefficient.

The key limitation in this study is due to sampling constraints when following the academic ethical guidelines, that state that underage citizens must not act as survey respondents or study objects. As illustrated in Figure 16 on page 40, the age distributions of each gender virtually resemble characteristics of a normal distribution, except for the omission of this age group. This clearly indicates that a significant proportion of study relevant participants have been neglected in this study, whose willingness to accept has not been captured here. A distorting influence is imaginable in both directions, as underage Instagram users may have less income and thus a lower WTA, however they may also irrationally value their account higher than older participants since social networks are deeply integrated into the daily lives of teenagers.

5.3   Outlook

The presented study convinces, especially in comparison with previous papers on related subjects, through a high fit with overall goodness criteria, sufficient sample size and representation of the suggested underlying user population regarding gender and age distribution.

Yet it is to note, that despite all efforts in this thesis, this analysis can only be considered a starting point for research on social media profile values and the resulting business models. Several starting points for future research shall briefly be presented here.

First of all given the high quality of the data sample, framed by the time constraints of this study, meta-analysis of the data is certainly an avenue that is worth pursuing in following studies. Regression analysis could be then carried out in depth with more variables, including an analysis of error terms in regards to a possible occurrence of heteroscedasticity. As the WTA instead of the WTP proved to be the more reliable construct to determine the account value, a second analysis of the WTA should be carried out in either meta analysis or within a new sample to validate the results of research question two and three and strengthen the position of this finding among researches.

Secondly quantitative research is becoming increasingly inconclusive when trying to look at examples and finding answers to less prevalent questions in research, like understanding why an Instagram account was created and the associated sentiments. Here it would be preferable to enhance the statistic heavy analysis through qualitative research, casting light on underlying motives and rationales. Further this would explain outliers, which may distort statistical data, but may hold important conclusions when users are analysed a second time in an interview scenario. Discussion or focus groups may lead to the development of case studies that can now be backed up with quantitative data from this study.

A stakeholder specific approach in later stages of research will also allow to address more specific and in depth questions on the actual insurance business model, the introduction of a Freemium model or practical guidelines for digital media agencies on pricing options on Instagram. Despite the apparent ethical concerns, future research should necessarily include the pivotal underage target group of Instagram users. In a larger scale study, written consent of parents and legal guardians, may be a viable option for researchers to collect data.

References

ACAR, G., VAN ALSENOY, B., PIESSENS, F., DIAZ, C. & PRENEEL, B. 2015. Facebook Tracking Through Social Plug-ins.

AHN, Y.-Y., HAN, S., KWAK, H., MOON, S. & JEONG, H. Analysis of topological characteristics of huge online social networking services. Proceedings of the 16th international conference on World Wide Web, 2007. ACM, 835-844.

AICHNER, T. & JACOB, F. 2015. Measuring the degree of corporate social media use. *International Journal of Market Research,* 57, 257-275.

AKERLOF, G. A. 1970. The market for" lemons": Quality uncertainty and the market mechanism. *The quarterly journal of economics,* 488-500.

AKERLOF, G. A. & KRANTON, R. E. 2000. Economics and identity. *Quarterly journal of Economics,* 715-753.

ALBRECHT, P. & MAURER, R. 2000. Zur bedeutung einer Ausfallbedrohtheit von Versicherungskontrakten—ein Beitrag zur Behavioral Insurance. *Zeitschrift für die gesamte Versicherungswissenschaft,* 89, 339-355.

ALEXA. 2015. *Alexa Top Rankings* [Online]. Alexa.com. Available: http://www.alexa.com/pro/dashboard/rankings [Accessed 19.5 2015].

ALHA, K., KOSKINEN, E., PAAVILAINEN, J., HAMARI, J. & KINNUNEN, J. 2014. Free-to-play games: Professionals' perspectives. *Proceedings of Nordic Digra.*

ANDERSON, C. 2009. The Future of a Radical Price. *New York.*

ANDERSON, D. R. 2001. The need to get the basics right in wildlife field studies. *Wildlife Society Bulletin,* 1294-1297.

ARMBRUST, M., FOX, A., GRIFFITH, R., JOSEPH, A. D., KATZ, R., KONWINSKI, A., LEE, G., PATTERSON, D., RABKIN, A. & STOICA, I. 2010. A view of cloud computing. *Communications of the ACM,* 53, 50-58.

ASHENFELTER, O. & JURAJDA, S. 2001. Cross-country comparisons of wage rates: The Big Mac index. *Unpublished paper, available at http://economics. uchicago. edu/download/bigmac. pdf.*

ATTESLANDER, P. 2003. *Methoden der empirischen Sozialforschung,* Walter de Gruyter.

AUSTER, C. J. & MANSBACH, C. S. 2012. The gender marketing of toys: An analysis of color and type of toy on the Disney store website. *Sex Roles,* 67, 375-388.

BAINS, M. 2014. *What is Amazon Cloud, Its Advantages and Why Should You Consider It - See more at: http://www.netsolutionsindia.com/blog/what-is-amazon-cloud-its-advantages-and-why-should-you-consider-it/#sthash.xQweTM3L.dpuf* [Online]. Available: http://www.netsolutionsindia.com/blog/what-is-amazon-cloud-its-advantages-and-why-should-you-consider-it/ [Accessed 2.8 2015].

BALLWIESER, W., BAMBERG, G., BECKMANN, M., BESTER, H., BLICKLE, M., EWERT, R., FEICHTINGER, G., FIRCHAU, V., FRICKE, F. & FUNKE, H. 2012. *Agency theory, information, and incentives*, Springer Science & Business Media.

BARRON, M. & TORERO, M. 2015. Fixed Costs, Spillovers, and Adoption of Electric Connections.

BAUER, C., KORUNOVSKA, J. & SPIEKERMANN, S. 2012. On the value of information-what Facebook users are willing to pay. *ECIS 2012 Proceedings*.

BECKER, C. & GUTSCHE, T. 2007. State-of-the-art von Auktionen.

BECKER, G. M., DEGROOT, M. H. & MARSCHAK, J. 1964. Measuring utility by a single–response sequential method. *Behavioral science*, 9, 226-232.

BEKKELUND, K. J. 2011. Succeeding with freemium. *Innovation and Entrepreneurship, Specialization Project*.

BERNINGHAUS, S. K., EHRHART, K.-M. & GÜTH, W. 2006. Auktionstheorie. *Strategische Spiele: Eine Einführung in die Spieltheorie*, 225-272.

BIERNACKI, P. & WALDORF, D. 1981. Snowball sampling: Problems and techniques of chain referral sampling. *Sociological methods & research*, 10, 141-163.

BOHNET, I. & ZECKHAUSER, R. 2004. Trust, risk and betrayal. *Journal of Economic Behavior & Organization*, 55, 467-484.

BORTZ, J. & DÖRING, N. 2006. *Forschungsmethoden und evaluation: für human-und sozialwissenschaftler*, Springer-Verlag.

BREIDERT, C., HAHSLER, M. & REUTTERER, T. 2006. A review of methods for measuring willingness-to-pay. *Innovative Marketing*, 2, 8-32.

BRUWER, J., SALIBA, A. & MILLER, B. 2011. Consumer behaviour and sensory preference differences: implications for wine product marketing. *Journal of Consumer Marketing*, 28, 5-18.

BÜHL, A. 2012. *SPSS 20: Einführung in die moderne Datenanalyse*, Pearson Deutschland GmbH.

BUNDESAMT, S. 2014. *Bildung, Forschung, Kultur*. Berlin: Statistisches Bundesamt.

CARLSSON, F. & MARTINSSON, P. 2001. Do hypothetical and actual marginal willingness to pay differ in choice experiments?: Application to the valuation of the environment. *Journal of Environmental Economics and Management*, 41, 179-192.

CHEN, Y. & TANG, F.-F. 1998. Learning and incentive-compatible mechanisms for public goods provision: An experimental study. *Journal of Political Economy*, 106, 633-662.

CORMODE, G. & KRISHNAMURTHY, B. 2008. Key differences between Web 1.0 and Web 2.0. *First Monday*, 13.

CRESWELL, J. W. 2013. *Research design: Qualitative, quantitative, and mixed methods approaches*, Sage publications.

CULLOTY, M. Twitter as a creative design tool: Inspiring creativity through microblog design aspects.

CUNNINGHAM, L. F., GERLACH, J. H., HARPER, M. D. & YOUNG, C. E. 2005. Perceived risk and the consumer buying process: internet airline reservations. *International Journal of Service Industry Management,* 16, 357-372.

DAVIS, D. D. & REILLY, R. J. 2012. On uncertainty and the WTA-WTP gap. *Economics Bulletin,* 32, 2594-2605.

DESREUMAUX, G. 2014. *The Complete History of Instagram* [Online]. WERSM. Available: http://wersm.com/the-complete-history-of-instagram/ [Accessed 2.8 2015].

DINEV, T. & HART, P. 2006. An Extended Privacy Calculus Model for E-Commerce Transactions. *Information Systems Research,* 17, 61-80.

DUBOURG, W. R., JONES-LEE, M. W. & LOOMES, G. 1994. Imprecise preferences and the WTP-WTA disparity. *Journal of Risk and Uncertainty,* 9, 115-133.

DUFRESNE, D. 1990. The distribution of a perpetuity, with applications to risk theory and pension funding. *Scandinavian Actuarial Journal,* 1990, 39-79.

EMARKETER. 2015. *Instagram Mobile Ad Revenues to Reach $2.81 Billion Worldwide in 2017* [Online]. Available: http://www.emarketer.com/Article/Instagram-Mobile-Ad-Revenues-Reach-281-Billion-Worldwide-2017/1012774 [Accessed 31.07 2015].

EXPLOARABLE. 2009. *Chain Referral Sampling* [Online]. Available: https://explorable.com/snowball-sampling [Accessed 12.8 2015].

FACEBOOK. 2012. *Facebook to Acquire Instagram* [Online]. Facebook Newsroom. Available: http://newsroom.fb.com/news/2012/04/facebook-to-acquire-instagram/ [Accessed 4.8 2015].

FARRELL, J. & SALONER, G. 1985. Standardization, compatibility, and innovation. *The RAND Journal of Economics,* 70-83.

FIEGERMAN, S. 2015. *Twitter really doesn't want its top users to share Instagram links anymore* [Online]. Available: http://mashable.com/2015/01/22/twitter-instagram-photos/ [Accessed 31.07 2015].

FISHBURN, P. C. & KOCHENBERGER, G. A. 1979. TWO–PIECE VON NEUMANN–MORGENSTERN UTILITY FUNCTIONS*. *Decision Sciences,* 10, 503-518.

FITTKAU&MAAS 2015. Fast jeder Dritte ist allein: In Deutschland leben mehr Singles als bisher bekannt. Hamburg: Marktforschungsinstitut Fittkau & Maaß.

FOX, G. & PIERCE, M. 2009. Grids challenged by a Web 2.0 and multicore sandwich. *Concurrency and Computation: Practice and Experience,* 21, 265-280.

GABEL, D. 1994. Competition in a network industry: the telephone industry, 1894–1910. *The journal of economic History,* 54, 543-572.

GEORGANTZIS, N. & NAVARRO-MARTÍNEZ, D. 2010. Understanding the WTA–WTP gap: Attitudes, feelings, uncertainty and personality. *Journal of Economic Psychology,* 31, 895-907.

GONDORF, L. 2015. *Altersunterschied zwischen Social-Media-Nutzern: Mit 18 bei Instagram, mit 30 auf Facebook* [Online]. Available: http://www.absatzwirtschaft.de/wer-nutzt-wirklich-facebook-snapchat-instagram-und-co-55345/ [Accessed 17.08 2015].

GOODMAN, R. & KISH, L. 1950. Controlled selection—a technique in probability sampling. *Journal of the American Statistical Association,* 45, 350-372.

GORDON, L. A., LOEB, M. P. & SOHAIL, T. 2003. A framework for using insurance for cyber-risk management. *Communications of the ACM,* 46, 81-85.

GROSSKLAGS, J. & ACQUISTI, A. When 25 Cents is Too Much: An Experiment on Willingness-To-Sell and Willingness-To-Protect Personal Information. WEIS, 2007.

GWI. 2014. *GWI Social Q4 2014* [Online]. GlobalWebIndex. Available: https://app.globalwebindex.net/products/report/gwi-social-q3-2014 [Accessed 18.5 2015].

HANN, I.-H., HUI, K. L., LEE, S.-Y. T. & PNG, I. P. Online Information Privacy: Measuring the Cost-Benefit Trade-Off. ICIS, 2002. 1.

HANNER, N. & ZARNEKOW, R. Purchasing Behavior in Free to Play Games: Concepts and Empirical Validation. System Sciences (HICSS), 2015 48th Hawaii International Conference on, 2015. IEEE, 3326-3335.

HERMANN, J. 2014. *Instagram Statistics* [Online]. Available: http://www.jennstrends.com/instagram-statistics-for-2014/ [Accessed 17.8 2015].

HESS, T., BANZERUS, A. & SCHREINER, M. 2014. ZB für Datenschutz als Freemium Modell. *WIM.*

HIGHAM, N. J. 2002. *Accuracy and stability of numerical algorithms,* Siam.

HONG, C. S., KARNI, E. & SAFRA, Z. 1987. Risk aversion in the theory of expected utility with rank dependent probabilities. *Journal of Economic theory,* 42, 370-381.

HOROWITZ, J. K. 2006. The Becker-DeGroot-Marschak mechanism is not necessarily incentive compatible, even for non-random goods. *Economics Letters,* 93, 6-11.

HOROWITZ, J. K. & MCCONNELL, K. E. 2000. The Endowment's Effect on Marginal Value. *Available at SSRN 261315.*

HOROWITZ, J. K. & MCCONNELL, K. E. 2002. A review of WTA/WTP studies. *Journal of Environmental Economics and Management,* 44, 426-447.

HOROWITZ, J. K. & MCCONNELL, K. E. 2003. Willingness to accept, willingness to pay and the income effect. *Journal of Economic Behavior & Organization,* 51, 537-545.

IBM 2013. IBM SPSS Statistics for Macintosh, Version 22.0. Armork, NY: IBM Corp.

ICONOSQUARE. 2015. *Statistics for your Instagram account* [Online]. Available: iconosquare.com/instagram-statistics [Accessed 21.05 2015].

INSTAGRAM. 2014. *Sponsored Photos and Videos* [Online]. Available: https://instagram.com/about-ads [Accessed 19.05 2015].

INSTAGRAM. 2015a. *Advertising* [Online]. Available: https://business.instagram.com/advertising/ [Accessed 4.8 2015].

INSTAGRAM. 2015b. *Main Page* [Online]. Available: http://instagram.com/ 2015].

INSTAGRAM. 2015c. *Teilen in sozialen Netzwerken* [Online]. Available: https://help.instagram.com/169948159813228/ [Accessed 31.7 2015].

ISIK, M. 2004. Does uncertainty affect the divergence between WTP and WTA measures? *Economics Bulletin,* 4, 1-7.

JOYCE, J. M. 2011. St. Petersburg Paradox. *International Encyclopedia of Statistical Science.* Springer.

KAAS, K. & RUPRECHT, H. 2006. Are the Vickrey auction and the BDM-mechanism really incentive compatible? Empirical results and optimal bidding strategies in the case of uncertain willingness-to-pay. *Empirical Results and Optimal Bidding Strategies in the Case of Uncertain Willingness-to-Pay.*

KAHNEMAN, D., KNETSCH, J. L. & THALER, R. H. 1991. Anomalies: The endowment effect, loss aversion, and status quo bias. *The journal of economic perspectives,* 193-206.

KAMBIL, A. 2008. What is your Web 5.0 strategy? *Journal of business strategy,* 29, 56-58.

KAPADIA, S. 2015. *Meet the UK women making thousands a month from Instagram and find out how to do it yourself* [Online]. Available: http://www.stylist.co.uk/fashion/make-money-internet-how-these-uk-british-women-are-making-a-living-off-instagram [Accessed 4.8 2015].

KAPLAN, A. M. & HAENLEIN, M. 2010. Users of the world, unite! The challenges and opportunities of Social Media. *Business horizons,* 53, 59-68.

KATONA, Z., ZUBCSEK, P. P. & SARVARY, M. 2011. Network effects and personal influences: The diffusion of an online social network. *Journal of marketing research,* 48, 425-443.

KATZ, M. L. & SHAPIRO, C. 1986. Technology adoption in the presence of network externalities. *The journal of political economy,* 822-841.

KELLER, L. R., SEGAL, U. & WANG, T. 1993. The Becker-DeGroot-Marschak mechanism and generalized utility theories: Theoretical predictions and empirical observations. *Theory and decision,* 34, 83-97.

KENDALL, M. G. 1938. A new measure of rank correlation. *Biometrika,* 81-93.

KHAZAAL, Y., VAN SINGER, M., CHATTON, A., ACHAB, S., ZULLINO, D., ROTHEN, S., KHAN, R., BILLIEUX, J. & THORENS, G. 2014. Does self-selection affect samples' representativeness in online surveys? An investigation in online video game research. *Journal of medical Internet research,* 16.

KIETZMANN, J. H., HERMKENS, K., MCCARTHY, I. P. & SILVESTRE, B. S. 2011. Social media? Get serious! Understanding the functional building blocks of social media. *Business horizons,* 54, 241-251.

KIM, H., HOUSE, L. A. & GAO, Z. 2012. Theoretical and Perceptual Market Values for Fresh Squeezed Orange Juice. *International Journal of Marketing Studies,* 4, p45.

KIRCHGÄSSNER, G. 2008. *Homo oeconomicus: Das ökonomische Modell individuellen Verhaltens und seine Anwendung in den Wirtschafts-und Sozialwissenschaften,* Mohr Siebeck.

KLEMPERER, P. 1987. Markets with consumer switching costs. *The quarterly journal of economics,* 375-394.

KNETSCH, J. L., TANG, F.-F. & THALER, R. H. 2001. The endowment effect and repeated market trials: Is the Vickrey auction demand revealing? *Experimental economics,* 4, 257-269.

KOSHAL, R. K. 1972. Economies of scale. *Journal of Transport Economics and Policy,* 147-153.

KRAHNEN, J. P., RIECK, C. & THEISSEN, E. 1997. Messung individueller Risikoeinstellungen. CFS Working Paper.

KROMREY, H. 2001. *Evaluation von Lehre und Studium–Anforderungen an Methodik und Design,* na.

KURAITIS, V. 2009. *What's a Network Industry?* [Online]. Available: http://e-caremanagement.com/whats-a-network-industry-is-healthcare-one/ [Accessed 19.05 2015].

KWAK, H., LEE, C., PARK, H. & MOON, S. What is Twitter, a social network or a news media? Proceedings of the 19th international conference on World wide web, 2010. ACM, 591-600.

LAUX, H. 2001. Bedingungen der Anreizkompatibilität, Fundierung von Unternehmenszielen und Anreize für deren Umsetzung. Working Paper Series: Finance & Accounting, Johann Wolfgang Goethe-Universität Frankfurt a. M.

LEADBEATER, C. Blog task 3a: Compare 3 Social networks–Pinterest, Instagram and Tumblr.

LEBER, J. 2012. *The Biggest Cost of Facebooks's Growth* [Online]. Available: http://www.technologyreview.com/news/427941/the-biggest-cost-of-facebooks-growth/ [Accessed 02.02 2014].

LEE, C., KUMAR, V. & GUPTA, S. 2013. Designing Freemium: a Model of Consumer Usage, Upgrade, and Referral Dynamics↩. Harvard Business School Working Paper.

LEE, C.-S. 2001. An analytical framework for evaluating e-commerce business models and strategies. *Internet Research,* 11, 349-359.

LEE, K., WEBB, S. & GE, H. 2015. Characterizing and automatically detecting crowdturfing in Fiverr and Twitter. *Social Network Analysis and Mining,* 5, 1-16.

LEFEVER, S., DAL, M. & MATTHIASDOTTIR, A. 2007. Online data collection in academic research: advantages and limitations. *British Journal of Educational Technology,* 38, 574-582.

LIN, K.-Y. & LU, H.-P. 2011. Why people use social networking sites: An empirical study integrating network externalities and motivation theory. *Computers in Human Behavior,* 27, 1152-1161.

LO, B. W. & SEDHAIN, R. S. 2006. How reliable are website rankings? Implications for e-business advertising and internet search. *Issues in Information Systems,* 7, 233-238.

LUSK, J. L. & SHOGREN, J. F. 2007. *Experimental Auctions: Methods and Applications in Economic and Marketing Research,* Cambridge University Press.

MA, H., WANG, X. H. & ZENG, C. 2015. Cournot and Bertrand Competition in a Differentiated Duopoly with Endogenous Technology Adoption. *ANNALS OF ECONOMICS AND FINANCE,* 16, 231-253.

MAJUMDAR, S. K. & VENKATARAMAN, S. 1998. Network effects and the adoption of new technology: evidence from the U. S. telecommunications industry. *Strategic Management Journal,* 19, 1045-1062.

MANNING, K. C., BEARDEN, W. O. & MADDEN, T. J. 1995. Consumer innovativeness and the adoption process. *Journal of Consumer Psychology,* 4, 329-345.

MARKUS, M. L. 1987. Toward a "critical mass" theory of interactive media universal access, interdependence and diffusion. *Communication research,* 14, 491-511.

MAS-COLELL, A., WHINSTON, M. D. & GREEN, J. R. 1995. *Microeconomic Theory,* Oxford University Press.

MASSEY JR, F. J. 1951. The Kolmogorov-Smirnov test for goodness of fit. *Journal of the American statistical Association,* 46, 68-78.

MILGROM, P. R. 2004. *Putting Auction Theory to Work,* Cambridge University Press.

MILLER, K. M. & HOFSTETTER, R. 2009. *Precision Pricing: Measuring Consumers' Willingness to Pay Accurately,* Books on Demand.

MILLER, K. M., HOFSTETTER, R., KROHMER, H. & ZHANG, Z. J. 2011. How should consumers' willingness to pay be measured? An empirical comparison of state-of-the-art approaches. *Journal of Marketing Research,* 48, 172-184.

MMU. 2015. *Ethical Framework* [Online]. Available: http://www2.mmu.ac.uk/research/ethics/ethics-forms-and-guidance/ [Accessed 25.5 2015].

MORIARTY, J. 2011. Qualitative methods overview.

MÜLLER, H., ERICHSON, B. & VOIGT, S. 2009. *Befragungsbasierte Methoden zur Ermittlung von Preisresponsefunktionen: Preisbereitschaft oder Kaufbereitschaft?*, Univ., FEMM.

NEUS, W. 2007. *Einführung in die Betriebswirtschaftslehre,* Tübingen, Mohr Siebeck Verlag.

NEUS, W. 2013. *Einführung in die Betriebswirtschaftslehre aus institutionenökonomischer Sicht,* Tübingen: Mohr Siebeck.

NOJIMA, M. 2007. Pricing models and motivations for MMO play. *Proceedings of DiGRA 2007,* 24-28.

NOUSSAIR, C., ROBIN, S. & RUFFIEUX, B. 2004. Revealing consumers' willingness-to-pay: A comparison of the BDM mechanism and the Vickrey auction. *Journal of economic psychology,* 25, 725-741.

O'REILLY, T. 2007. What is Web 2.0: Design patterns and business models for the next generation of software. *Communications & strategies,* 17.

O'REILLY, T. 2005. Web 2.0: Compact Definition?(2005). O'Reilly Radar. Electronic document. Date of publication: October.

OKADA, E. M. 2010. Uncertainty, risk aversion, and WTA vs. WTP. *Marketing Science,* 29, 75-84.

ONG, L. L. 1997. Burgernomics: the economics of the Big Mac standard. *Journal of International Money and Finance,* 16, 865-878.

OTTUM, B. D. & MOORE, W. L. 1997. The role of market information in new product success/failure. *Journal of Product Innovation Management,* 14, 258-273.

PAE, S. 2005. Selective disclosures in the presence of uncertainty about information endowment. *Journal of Accounting and Economics,* 39, 383-409.

PATTERSON, M. 2015. *Social Media Demographics for Marketers* [Online]. Available: http://sproutsocial.com/insights/new-social-media-demographics/ [Accessed 17.8 2015].

PAUL, T., PUSCHER, D. & STRUFE, T. 2015. Private Date Exposure in Facebook and the Impact of Comprehensible Audience Selection Controls. *arXiv preprint arXiv:1505.06178.*

PERREY, J. & SPILLECKE, D. 2013. *Retail Marketing and Branding: A Definitive Guide to Maximizing ROI,* Wiley.

POLASEK, W. 2013. *EDA Explorative datenanalyse: einführung in die deskriptive Statistik,* Springer-Verlag.

PUYOL, N. 2010. Freemium: attributes of an emerging business model. *Social Science Research Network.*

QUALTRICS, L. 2014. Qualtrics [software].

RIECK, C. 2010. Spieltheorie. 10. *Auflage, Wiesbaden.*

ROGERS, E. M. 2010. *Diffusion of innovations*, Simon and Schuster.

ROSSI, P. H., WRIGHT, J. D. & ANDERSON, A. B. 2013. *Handbook of survey research*, Academic Press.

SAYMAN, S. & ÖNCÜLER, A. 2005. Effects of study design characteristics on the WTA–WTP disparity: A meta analytical framework. *Journal of economic psychology,* 26, 289-312.

SCHMIDT, F. L. & HUNTER, J. E. 2014. *Methods of Meta-Analysis: Correcting Error and Bias in Research Findings*, SAGE Publications.

SCHOGER, C. 2013. DISTIMO 2013 Year in Review.

SCHREINER, M. & HESS, T. On The Willingness To Pay For Privacy As A Freemium Model: First Empirical Evidence. ECIS, 2013a. 30.

SCHREINER, M. & HESS, T. 2013b. On The Willingness To Pay For Privacy As A Freemium Model: First Empirical Evidence.

SCHREINER, M. & HESS, T. 2015. Why Are Consumers Willing to Pay for Privacy? An Application of the Privacy-freemium Model to Media Companies.

SCHRÖDER, J. 2014. *Top 20 der sozialen Netzwerke in Deutschland: Twitter, Instagram und Reddit die großen Gewinner* [Online]. Available: http://meedia.de/2014/11/05/top-20-der-sozialen-netzwerke-in-deutschland-twitter-instagram-und-reddit-die-grossen-gewinner/.

SCHUMPETER, J. A. 1984. The meaning of rationality in the social sciences. *Zeitschrift für die gesamte Staatswissenschaft/Journal of Institutional and Theoretical Economics,* 577-593.

SHAPIRO, C. & VARIAN, H. R. 2013. *Information rules: a strategic guide to the network economy*, Harvard Business Press.

SHOGREN, J. F., MARGOLIS, M., KOO, C. & LIST, J. A. 2001. A random nth-price auction. *Journal of economic behavior & organization,* 46, 409-421.

SHOGREN, J. F., SHIN, S. Y., HAYES, D. J. & KLIEBENSTEIN, J. B. 1994. Resolving differences in willingness to pay and willingness to accept. *The American Economic Review,* 255-270.

SHRIVER, S. K. 2015. Network effects in alternative fuel adoption: Empirical analysis of the market for ethanol. *Marketing Science,* 34, 78-97.

SHY, O. 2001. *The economics of network industries*, Cambridge University Press.

SIEGLER, M. 2010. *Burbn's Funding Goes Down Smooth. Baseline, Andreessen Back Stealthy Location Startup.* [Online]. Available: http://techcrunch.com/2010/03/05/burbn-funding/ [Accessed 4.8 2015].

SILVA, A., NAYGA JR, R. M., CAMPBELL, B. L. & PARK, J. 2007. On the use of valuation mechanisms to measure consumers' willingness to pay for novel products: A comparison of hypothetical and non-hypothetical values. *International Food and Agribusiness Management Review,* 10, 165-180.

SIMON, H. & FASSNACHT, M. 2008. *Preismanagement: Strategie-Analyse-Entscheidung-Umsetzung*, Springer DE.

SIMPLYMEASURED. 2015. *Instagram Analytics Tool* [Online]. Available: simplymeasured.com/freebies/instagram-analytics [Accessed 21.5 2015].

SKIERA, B. 1999. *Mengenbezogene Preisdifferenzierung bei Diestleistungen,* Wiesbaden.

SMITH, C. 2014. *The Programmatic Advertising Report* [Online]. Available: http://www.businessinsider.com/instagram-demographics-2013-12?IR=T [Accessed 11.8 2015].

SMITH, H. J., MILBERG, S. J. & BURKE, S. J. 1996. Information Privacy: Measuring Individuals' Concerns About Organizational Practices. *MIS quarterly,* 20.

SPANNAUS, D. 2014. *Fast 10 Mio. Twitter Nutzer in Deutschland – und keiner hat es gemerkt?* [Online]. twentyZen. Available: http://www.twentyzen.com/de/fast-10-mio-twitter-nutzer-in-deutschland/ [Accessed 11.08 2015].

STÄHLER, P. 2002. *Geschäftsmodelle in der digitalen Ökonomie: Merkmale, Strategien und Auswirkungen,* Eul.

STATISTA. 2015a. *Distribution of Instagram users in the United States as of January 2015, by age group* [Online]. Available: http://www.statista.com/statistics/398166/us-instagram-user-age-distribution/ [Accessed 17.08 2015].

STATISTA. 2015b. *Fakten zum Thema: Durchschnittseinkommen* [Online]. Available: http://de.statista.com/themen/293/durchschnittseinkommen/ [Accessed 18.8 2015].

STATISTA. 2015c. *Monthly active Useres of Instagram* [Online]. Available: http://www.statista.com/statistics/282087/number-of-monthly-active-twitter-users/ [Accessed 31.7 2015].

STECKLER, A., MCLEROY, K. R., GOODMAN, R. M., BIRD, S. T. & MCCORMICK, L. 1992. Toward integrating qualitative and quantitative methods: an introduction. *Health education quarterly,* 19, 1-8.

STEINER, M. & HENDUS, J. 2012. How Consumers' Willingness to Pay is Measured in Practice: An Empirical Analysis of Common Approaches' Relevance. *Available at SSRN 2025618.*

STRUTTON, M. J., ESTES, C., FOSSAN, S., THOMPSON, E., WOODS, S. K. & SHEIKH, T. 2014. Method and system for integrating audience data with a social media site. Google Patents.

SYSTROM, K. 2010. *What is the genesis of Instagram?* [Online]. Available: http://www.quora.com/What-is-the-genesis-of-Instagram [Accessed 2.8 2015].

TADDICKEN, M. 2014. The 'Privacy Paradox'in the Social Web: The Impact of Privacy Concerns, Individual Characteristics, and the Perceived Social Relevance on Different Forms of Self–Disclosure. *Journal of Computer–Mediated Communication,* 19, 248-273.

TECHCRUNCH. 2010. *Burbn's Funding Goes Down Smooth. Baseline, Andreessen Back Stealthy Location Startup.* [Online]. Available:

http://techcrunch.com/2010/03/05/burbn-funding/ [Accessed 20.5 2015].

THOMAS, H. 2012. *Instagram for Android now available* [Online]. Available: http://www.theverge.com/2012/4/3/2922607/instagram-for-android-available-in-google-play-store [Accessed 4.8 2015].

TOUTENBURG, H. & HEUMANN, C. 2008. *Deskriptive Statistik: eine Einführung in Methoden und Anwendungen mit R und SPSS*, Springer-Verlag.

TUCKER, C. E. 2014. Social networks, personalized advertising, and privacy controls. *Journal of Marketing Research,* 51, 546-562.

TURBAN, E., KING, D., LEE, J. K., LIANG, T.-P. & TURBAN, D. C. 2015. *Electronic commerce: A managerial and social networks perspective*, Springer.

UCLA. 2015. *U.S. National Surveys* [Online]. Available: http://www.sscnet.ucla.edu/issr/da/Home.NatSurveys.htm [Accessed 20.5 2015].

UDO, G. J. 2001. Privacy and security concerns as major barriers for e-commerce: a survey study. *Information Management & Computer Security,* 9, 165-174.

VAIDYANATHAN, G. & DEVARAJ, S. 2003. A five-factor framework for analyzing online risks in e-businesses. *Communications of the ACM,* 46, 354-361.

VALENTE, T. W. 1995. *Network models of the diffusion of innovations*, Hampton Press Cresskill, NJ.

VALENTE, T. W. 1996. Social network thresholds in the diffusion of innovations. *Social networks,* 18, 69-89.

VAN MIERLO, T. 2014. The 1% rule in four digital health social networks: an observational study. *Journal of medical Internet research,* 16.

VAN WESTENDORP, P. H. NSS Price Sensitivity Meter (PSM)–A new approach to study consumer perception of prices. ESOMAR Congress (25 th) Venice, 1976. 139-166.

VICKREY, W. 1961. Counterspeculation, auctions, and competitive sealed tenders. *The Journal of finance,* 16, 8-37.

VON NEUMANN, J. & MORGENSTERN, O. 2007. *Theory of games and economic behavior (60th Anniversary Commemorative Edition)*, Princeton university press.

VON NITZSCH, R. 2006. *Entscheidungslehre*, Mainz.

WALTER, S., ELIASZIW, M. & DONNER, A. 1998. Sample size and optimal designs for reliability studies. *Statistics in medicine,* 101-10.

WANG, Y. & HAJLI, M. N. Co-creation in branding through social commerce: The role of social support, relationship quality and privacy concerns. Proceedings of Twentieth Americas Conference on Information Systems, Savannah, Georgia, 2014.

WEINBERG, T. 2009. *The new community rules: Marketing on the social web*, O'Reilly Sebastopol, CA.

WERTENBROCH, K. & SKIERA, B. 2002. Measuring consumers' willingness to pay at the point of purchase. *Journal of Marketing Research,* 39, 228-241.

WILSON, F. 2006. *The Freemium Business Model* [Online]. Available: http://www.avc.com/a_vc/2006/03/the_freemium_bu.html [Accessed Feb 2 2014].

WRIGHT, K. B. 2005. Researching Internet–based populations: Advantages and disadvantages of online survey research, online questionnaire authoring software packages, and web survey services. *Journal of Computer–Mediated Communication,* 10, 00-00.

ZAPPAVIGNA, M. & ZHAO, S. Seminar on Personal digital photographic practices on Instagram & Tumblr.

ZEILER, K. & PLOTT, C. R. 2004. The willingness to pay/willingness to accept gap, the endowment effect, subject misconceptions and experimental procedures for eliciting valuations. *American Economic Review.*

ZHAO, J. & KLING, C. L. 2001. A new explanation for the WTP/WTA disparity. *Economics Letters,* 73, 293-300.

ZIKMUND, W., BABIN, B., CARR, J. & GRIFFIN, M. 2012. *Business research methods*, Cengage Learning.

Appendices

Appendix 1: Criteria for a market of lemons (Akerlof, 1970)

"The Market for Lemons: Quality Uncertainty and the Market Mechanism" is a paper by George Akerlof (1970), which stress the effects of asymmetric in-formation between the seller and the buyer of a product or service. The original issue of quality differences in the market for used cars can appropriately be transferred to the photo-sharing service Instagram. Moreover, Akerlof's assumptions are likely to be accurate for transactions regarding sponsored posts on the social network Instagram:

1. Asymmetric information is present as no advertising firm may exactly quantify the benefit that could be derived from a sponsored posed from an unknown user.
2. An incentive for the Instagram user exists to sell low-quality advertising space as a higher-quality advertising space (e.g. using fake followers).
3. Disclosure technologies (e.g. online ratings) are not available for advertising firms.
4. The average quality of offered sponsored posts is considered to be low.
5. Effective guarantees, regulation or warranties are usually not available.

Appendix 2: Approximation of $(E(\Delta N_F))$ based on the history of two Instagram accounts

Account 1: 6686 Follower

Lower border: Decrease of N_F by 3 Followers = 0.00044 $\approx$ 0.04%

Upper border: Decrease of N_F by 20 Followers = 0.00299 $\approx$ 0.30%

Account 2: 15051 Follower

Lower border: Decrease of N_F by 6 Followers = 0.00039 $\approx$ 0.04%

Upper border: Decrease of N_F by 45 Followers = 0.00298 $\approx$ 0.30%

Appendix 3: Both Instagram accounts benefit from sponsored posts

Example 1:

An individual owns an Instagram Account with 1000 Followers (Ashenfelter and Jurajda) and an overall assessed WTA of 1500 €, where sponsored posts are offered on the market. He expected that his number of followers per advertisement post (by people who feel annoyed of the advertisement) drop by 5 people $(E(\Delta N_F))$ and thus inserted as -5 in the formula. The individual risk premium is equal to 1 € and based on the fact that the expected change in the number of followers is not precisely predictable. The correlation between the number of followers and the WTA is 0.7 $(r_{NF;WTA})$. [12]

$$p^* = \left(\frac{+5}{1000} \times 0.7 \times 1500€\right) + 1$$

$$p^* = 6.25 €$$

Consequently, he should ask for 6.25 € for per sponsored post

Example 2:

An individual owns an Instagram Account with 1000 Followers (Ashenfelter and Jurajda) and an overall assessed WTA of 1500 €, where sponsored posts are offered on the market. He expected that his number of followers per advertisement post increase by 10 followers through increased reputation or maybe even a link on the companies page. The individual risk premium is equal to 1 € and based on the fact that the expected change in the number of followers is not precisely predictable. The correlation between the number of followers and the WTA is assumed to be 0.7 $(r_{NF};WTA)$.

$$p^* = \left(\frac{-10}{1000} \times 0.7 \times 1500€\right) + 1$$

$$p^* = -9.5€$$

As a consequence, the user should be willing to pay 9.5 € for engaging in the business cooperation regarding sponsored posts, as the individual account value (WTA) is expected to increase.

---

[12] Assumption: calculation of this constant occurs in section 4.

Appendix 4: Survey

Online Survey:

https://qtrial2015az1.az1.qualtrics.com/SE/?SID=SV_aWQ9vhc1KZLCj7T

Paper-Based Survey (English version):

Thank you for taking the time to answer this survey and enable valuable insights for my Master thesis and future publication at the Manchester Metropolitan University. Your answers will be completely anonymous and will not be passed to third parties. If you have any questions about the survey, feel free to contact me at: andreas.a.banzerus@stu.mmu.ac.uk

Estimated time: **5 min**

Q1 Gender

○ Male
○ Female

Q2 Age

Q3 In which country is your (main) residence?

Q4 What is your martial status?

○ Single
○ Life Partner
○ Married

Q5 What is the highest level of education you have completed?

○ No formal qualifications
○ GCSEs or equivalent qualifications (Senior School)
○ A-levels or equivalent qualifications (High School)
○ Bachelors degree, equivalent and higher qualifications
○ Other qualifications (including foreign qualifications)

Q6 What is your annual income range?

○ Below 10,000
○ 10,000 - 29,999
○ 30,000 - 49,999
○ 50,000 - 69,999
○ Above 70,000

Q8 Number of Followers on Instagram (please give exact figures).

Q9 Number of Accounts you follow on Instagram (please give exact figures).

Q10 Posted Photos in total (please give exact figures).

Q11 When did you sign up on Instagram?

○ 2010   ○ 2013

○ 2011   ○ 2014

○ 2012   ○ 2015

Q12 Estimate the average number of likes per photo/video.

Q13 Estimate the average number of comments per photo/video.

Q14 To which categories do most of your pictures relate to? (You may select multiple categories)

○ Fashion

○ Travel

○ Beauty

○ Technology and Electronics

○ Food

○ Sports and Fitness

○ Personal and Diary

○ Professional Photography

○ Other

Q15a Have you ever engaged in a business cooperation on Instagram? (e.g. marketing, promotion, sponsored content,...)?

○ Yes
○ No

Q15b Have you ever received free products following promotional activities?

○ Yes
○ No

Q15c Have you ever received money following promotional activities?
○ Yes
○ No

Q14b How much do you earn a month due to activities on Instagram? (in your local currency)

Q15 State your price at which you would delete your current Instagram account:

To ensure the overall quality of this study you can now (voluntarily) state the name of your Instagram Account.

Account Name: | |

According to MMU's Privacy Policy gathered data will not be distributed to third parties.

Appendix 5

Variable name	Type	Width	Decimals	Values	Measure
user	numeric	1	0	1 = user 2 = no user	nominal
sex	numeric	1	0	0 = male 1 = female	nominal
age	numeric	2	0		scale
country	numeric	3	0	9 = Australia 10 = Austria 20 = Bhutan 26 = Bulgaria 57 = Estonia 65 = Germany 94 = Latvia 120 = Nauru 128 = Norway 130 = Pakistan 143 = Russia 169 = Switzerland 179 = Turkey 185 = UK 187 = USA	nominal
maritial	numeric	1	0	1 = Single 2 =Life Partner 3 = Married 4 = Divorced 5 = Widowed	nominal
education_uk	numeric	1	0	1 = No formal qualifications 2 = GCSEs (Senior School) 3 = A-level (High School) 4 = Bachelors degree 5 = Other qualifications (e.g foreign)	ordinal
education_ger	numeric	1	0	1 = No formal qualifications 2 = Hauptschulabschluss 3 = Realschulabschluss 4 = Ausbildung 5 = Hochschulreife 6 = Bachelors degree 7 = Other qualifications (e.g. foreign)	
income	numeric	1	0	1 = Below 10,000 2 = 10,000 – 29,999 3 = 30,000 – 49,999 4 = 50,000 – 69,999 5 = Above 70,000	ordinal
followers	numeric	6	0		scale
followings	numeric	4	0		scale
posts	numeric	4	0		scale
since	numeric	1	0	1 = 2015 2 = 2014 3 = 2013 4 = 2012 5 = 2011 6 = 2010	ordinal

likes_avg	numeric	5	0		scale
comments_avg	numeric	4	0		scale
category	numeric	1	0	1 = Fashion 2 = Travel 3 = Beauty 4 = Technology and Electronics 5 = Food 6 = Sports and Fitness 7 = Personal and Diary 8 = Professional Photography 9 = Other	nominal
business	numeric	1	0	1 = Yes 2 = No	nominal
business_product	numeric	1	0	1 = Yes 2 = No	nominal
business_money	numeric	1	0	1 = Yes 2 = No	nominal
business_income	numeric	4	0		scale
wta	numeric	6	1		scale
wta_2	numeric	1	0	1 = Below 10 2 = 10 – 99 3 = 100 – 999 4 = 1,000 – 9,999 5 = 10,000 – 99,999 6 = Above 100,000	ordinal

Missing values were coded as -1, if present.

Appendix 6

Chi-Square Test

Frequencies

sex

	Observed N	Expected N	Residual
male	93	204,5	−111,5
female	316	204,5	111,5
Total	409		

Test Statistics

	sex
Chi-Square	121,587[a]
df	1
Asymp. Sig.	,000

a. 0 cells (0,0%) have expected frequencies less than 5. The minimum expected cell frequency is 204,5.

Appendix 7

country

N	Valid	409
	Missing	0
Mode		65

country

		Frequency	Percent	Valid Percent	Cumulative Percent
Valid	Australia	2	,5	,5	,5
	Austria	21	5,1	5,1	5,6
	Bhutan	1	,2	,2	5,9
	Bulgaria	1	,2	,2	6,1
	Estonia	1	,2	,2	6,4
	Germany	356	87,0	87,0	93,4
	Latvia	1	,2	,2	93,6
	Nauru	1	,2	,2	93,9
	Norway	1	,2	,2	94,1
	Pakistan	1	,2	,2	94,4
	Russia	1	,2	,2	94,6
	Switzerland	1	,2	,2	94,9
	Turkey	1	,2	,2	95,1
	United Kingdom	19	4,6	4,6	99,8
	United States	1	,2	,2	100,0
	Total	409	100,0	100,0	

Appendix 8

Test Statistics

	martial
Chi-Square	64,635[a]
df	4
Asymp. Sig.	,000

a. 2 cells (40,0%) have expected frequencies less than 5. The minimum expected cell frequency is 4,1.

Appendix 9

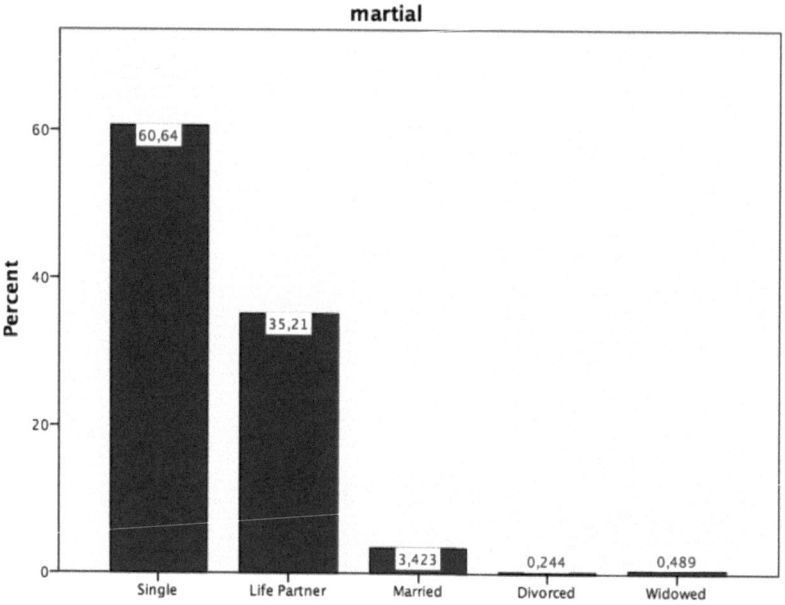

martial

Appendix 10

education_uk

		Frequency	Percent	Valid Percent	Cumulative Percent
Valid	No formal qualifications	1	,2	1,9	1,9
	GCSEs or equivalent qualifications (Senior School)	3	,7	5,7	7,5
	A–levels or equivalent qualifications (High School)	22	5,4	41,5	49,1
	Bachelors degree, equivalent and higher qualifications	24	5,9	45,3	94,3
	Other qualifications (including foreign qualifications)	3	,7	5,7	100,0
	Total	53	13,0	100,0	
Missing	System	356	87,0		
Total		409	100,0		

education_ger

		Frequency	Percent	Valid Percent	Cumulative Percent
Valid	No formal qualifications	5	1,2	1,4	1,4
	Hauptschulabschluss	8	2,0	2,2	3,7
	Realschulabschluss	16	3,9	4,5	8,1
	Ausbildung	10	2,4	2,8	11,0
	Fachhochschulreife / Allgem. Hochschulreife	242	59,2	68,0	78,9
	Bachelors degree or equivalent and higher qualifications	71	17,4	19,9	98,9
	Other qualifications (including foreign qualifications)	4	1,0	1,1	100,0
	Total	356	87,0	100,0	
Missing	System	53	13,0		
Total		409	100,0		

Appendix 11

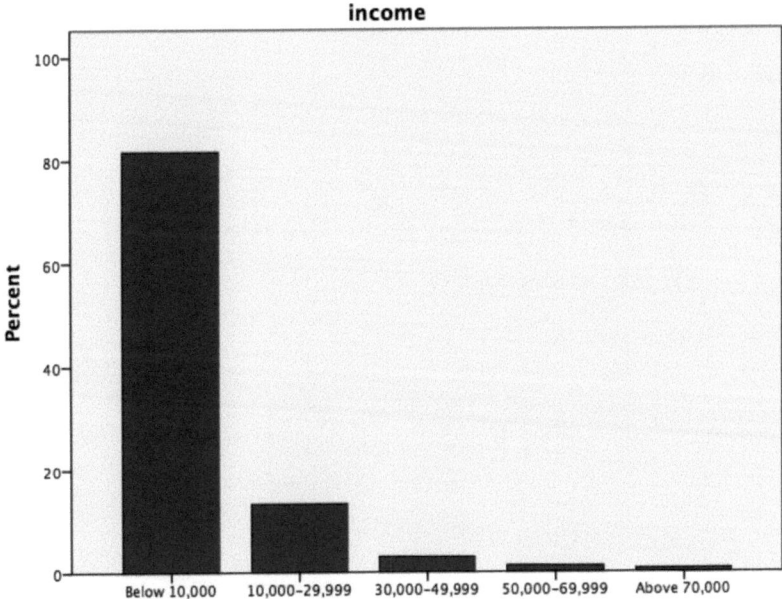

income

Appendix 12

since		
N	Valid	409
	Missing	0
Mean		2,72
Median		3,00
Mode		3
Std. Deviation		1,094
Minimum		1
Maximum		6

Appendix 13

		likes_avg	comments_avg
N	Valid	409	409
	Missing	0	0
Mean		90,68	18,92
Median		20,00	2,00
Mode		20	1
Std. Deviation		586,986	279,071
Minimum		0	0
Maximum		10000	5626

Appendix 14

		Fashion	Travel	Beauty	Technology	Food	Sports	Personal	Photography	Other
N=409	Sum	89	206	53	7	137	80	220	27	63
	Percent	21,8	50,4	13,0	1,7	33,5	19,6	53,8	6,6	15,4

Appendix 15

business			
		Frequency	Percent
Valid	Yes	33	8,1
	No	376	91,9
	Total	409	100,0

Appendix 16

business_product

		Frequency	Percent	Valid Percent	Cumulative Percent
Valid	Yes	16	3,9	48,5	48,5
	No	17	4,2	51,5	100,0
	Total	33	8,1	100,0	
Missing	System	376	91,9		
Total		409	100,0		

business_money

		Frequency	Percent	Valid Percent	Cumulative Percent
Valid	Yes	6	1,5	19,4	19,4
	No	25	6,1	80,6	100,0
	Total	31	7,6	100,0	
Missing	System	378	92,4		
Total		409	100,0		

Appendix 17

business_income

		Frequency	Percent	Valid Percent
Valid	5	1	,2	20,0
	30	1	,2	20,0
	42	1	,2	20,0
	500	1	,2	20,0
	1000	1	,2	20,0
	Total	5	1,2	100,0
Missing	System	404	98,8	
Total		409	100,0	

Appendix 18

WTA

N	Valid	409
	Missing	0
Mean		2850927,16
Median		100,0000
Mode		100,00
Std. Deviation		50682479,8
Minimum		,00
Maximum		1,00E+9

Appendix 19

Case Processing Summary

	Cases					
	Valid		Missing		Total	
	N	Percent	N	Percent	N	Percent
WTA	393	84,7%	71	15,3%	464	100,0%

Descriptives

			Statistic	Std. Error
WTA	Mean		2850927,16	2556592,91
	95% Confidence Interval for Mean	Lower Bound	-2175421,7	
		Upper Bound	7877276,02	
	5% Trimmed Mean		615,9580	
	Median		100,0000	
	Variance		2,569E+15	
	Std. Deviation		50682479,8	
	Minimum		,00	
	Maximum		1,00E+009	
	Range		1,00E+9	
	Interquartile Range		450,00	
	Skewness		19,545	,123
	Kurtosis		385,136	,246

M-Estimators

	Huber's M-Estimator[a]	Tukey's Biweight[b]	Hampel's M-Estimator[c]	Andrews' Wave[d]
WTA	145,1952	75,3443	102,5888	74,4152

a. The weighting constant is 1,339.
b. The weighting constant is 4,685.
c. The weighting constants are 1,700, 3,400, and 8,500.
d. The weighting constant is 1,340*pi.

Percentiles

		Percentiles					
		5	10	25	50	75	90
Weighted Average (Definition 1)	WTA	1,0000	7,0000	50,0000	100,0000	500,0000	2500,0000
Tukey's Hinges	WTA			50,0000	100,0000	500,0000	

Percentiles

		Percentiles
		95
Weighted Average (Definition 1)	WTA	10000,0000
Tukey's Hinges	WTA	

Extreme Values

		Case Number	Value
WTA	Highest	301	1,00E+009
		276	1,00E+008
		255	1,00E+007
		369	5,00E+006
		8	1,00E+006[a]

a. Only a partial list of cases with the value 1,00E+006 are shown in the table of upper extremes.

Box plot:

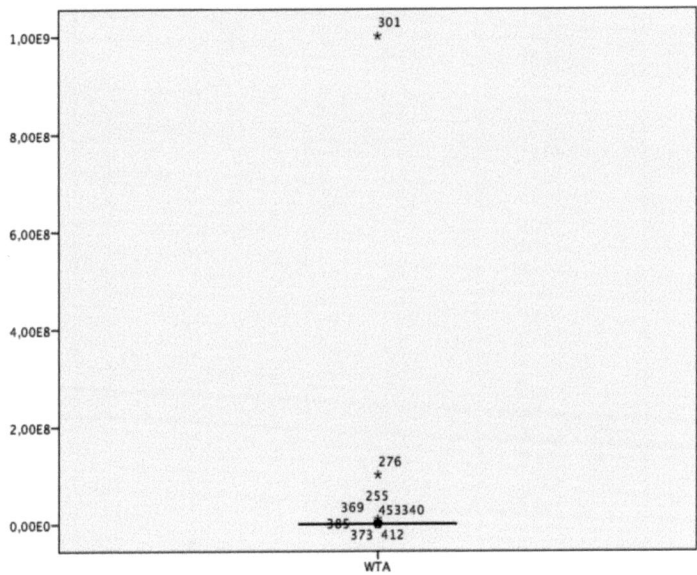

wta

		Frequency	Percent	Valid Percent	Cumulative Percent
Valid	,0	11	2,7	2,8	2,8
	1,0	13	3,2	3,3	6,2
	2,0	2	,5	,5	6,7
	4,0	1	,2	,3	6,9
	5,0	12	2,9	3,1	10,0
	10,0	20	4,9	5,1	15,2
	15,0	5	1,2	1,3	16,5
	20,0	19	4,6	4,9	21,3
	25,0	6	1,5	1,5	22,9
	30,0	3	,7	,8	23,7
	40,0	4	1,0	1,0	24,7
	50,0	47	11,5	12,1	36,8
	60,0	2	,5	,5	37,3
	70,0	2	,5	,5	37,8
	75,0	1	,2	,3	38,0
	80,0	2	,5	,5	38,6
	80,5	1	,2	,3	38,8
	99,0	1	,2	,3	39,1
	100,0	61	14,9	15,7	54,8
	120,0	2	,5	,5	55,3
	140,0	1	,2	,3	55,5
	150,0	7	1,7	1,8	57,3
	155,0	1	,2	,3	57,6
	200,0	22	5,4	5,7	63,2
	250,0	8	2,0	2,1	65,3
	300,0	5	1,2	1,3	66,6
	350,0	3	,7	,8	67,4
	400,0	3	,7	,8	68,1
	450,0	1	,2	,3	68,4
	500,0	41	10,0	10,5	78,9
	600,0	3	,7	,8	79,7
	700,0	2	,5	,5	80,2
	800,0	2	,5	,5	80,7
	1000,0	31	7,6	8,0	88,7
	1227,0	1	,2	,3	88,9
	2000,0	10	2,4	2,6	91,5
	2001,0	1	,2	,3	91,8
	2500,0	2	,5	,5	92,3
	3000,0	2	,5	,5	92,8
	3500,0	1	,2	,3	93,1
	5000,0	10	2,4	2,6	95,6
	10000,0	15	3,7	3,9	99,5
	250000,0	1	,2	,3	99,7
	500000,0	1	,2	,3	100,0
	Total	389	95,1	100,0	
Missing	-1,0	10	2,4		
	System	10	2,4		
	Total	20	4,9		
Total		409	100,0		

Appendix 21

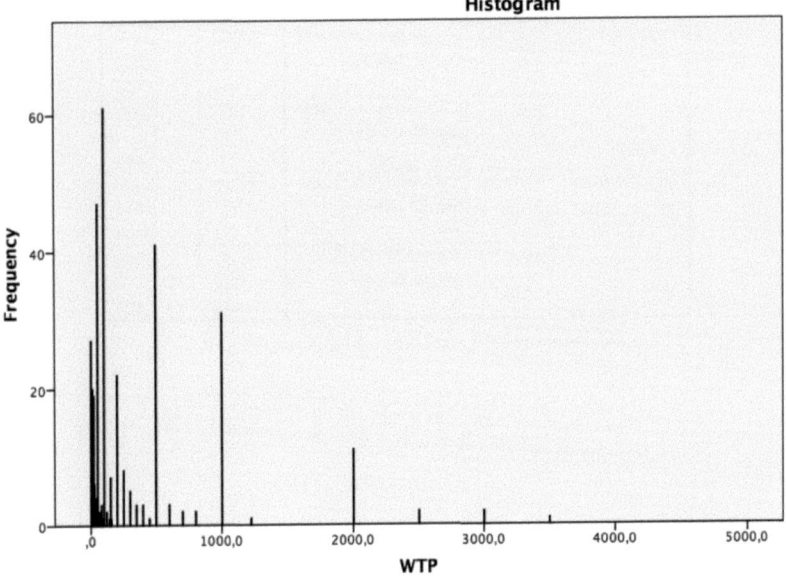

Appendix 22

			wta
Kendall's tau_b	sex	Correlation Coefficient	,042
		Sig. (2-tailed)	,326
		N	389
	country	Correlation Coefficient	-,014
		Sig. (2-tailed)	,737
		N	389
	martial	Correlation Coefficient	,008
		Sig. (2-tailed)	,852
		N	389
	education_uk	Correlation Coefficient	-,015
		Sig. (2-tailed)	,898
		N	48
	education_ger	Correlation Coefficient	,022
		Sig. (2-tailed)	,611
		N	341
	income	Correlation Coefficient	,098
		Sig. (2-tailed)	,022
		N	379

Appendix 23

			business	wta
Kendall's tau_b	business	Correlation Coefficient	1,000	-,107[*]
		Sig. (2-tailed)	.	,013
		N	409	409
	wta	Correlation Coefficient	-,107[*]	1,000
		Sig. (2-tailed)	,013	.
		N	409	409
Spearman's rho	business	Correlation Coefficient	1,000	-,127[*]
		Sig. (2-tailed)	.	,012
		N	409	409
	wta	Correlation Coefficient	-,127[*]	1,000
		Sig. (2-tailed)	,012	.
		N	409	409

*. Correlation is significant at the 0.05 level (2-tailed).